EXCELLENCE *in* EXECUTION

EXCELLENCE *in* EXECUTION

"Given the increasing uncertainty and complexity in world markets today, the ongoing dynamic interplay between strategy and execution becomes critical. *Excellence in Execution* provides a wealth of practical and actionable resources to ensure that your organization's evolving strategy can be effectively and efficiently executed. Robin Speculand has always been ahead of the curve when it comes to strategy execution, and his new book could not be more timely. Ignore it at your own peril."

— **Dr. Tony O'Driscoll**, Global Head of
Strategic Leadership Solutions, Duke CE

"Growing a business such as YCH Group requires more than just strategic thinking. It requires executives to have a shared understanding of the strategy and to then translate and execute it within their respective focus areas. This book is an indispensable companion for any business, regardless of size and structure, to systematically implement their strategy in an orchestrated manner."

— **Dr. Robert Yap**, Executive Chairman, YCH Group

"You will enjoy discovering the tale, the inside story of the case studies, along with the thoughts of Robin Speculand, a pioneer and expert in how to implement strategy. You will be introduced to highly practical toolkits, checklists and templates of tremendous interest if you want to be excellent in efficient execution of your strategy. Let yourself be charmed by the ideas, practical techniques and in-depth stories proposed by Robin Speculand."

— **Yves Pigneur**, Professor, University of Lausanne,
Co-author, international bestseller *Business Model Generation*

"Going from strategy to performance is hard: Most companies don't spend nearly as much time on how to get there as on crafting their strategies. *Excellence in Execution* maps out a step-by-step approach for how *not* to get stuck with a perfect plan that is imperfectly executed. Full of toolkits and checklists, this book is a definitive, comprehensive guide of how to deal with the Achilles heel of strategy: strategy execution."

— **Serguei Netessine**, Timken Chaired Professor of Global Technology and Innovation, INSEAD, Author, *The Risk-Driven Business Model*

"Overseeing Asia Pacific, I am constantly challenged with ensuring the multiple business units in the region are implementing specific corporate strategies, with consistent set of performance goals, customer engagement, and operating models. From the point when IDC engaged Robin on a consulting project, we are reminded that strategy is of little value unless it can be acted upon. I was delighted to read the depth of new thinking, material and tools in this book. It is very much a 'how to' that is missing in business today. Robin has filled this much needed space."

— **Eva Au**, Managing Director, IDC Asia/Pacific

"Robin Speculand has devoted his global career to helping leaders convert strategy into valuable business results. The key to their success—and yours—is execution. In this new book, Robin details HOW to execute strategy with a wealth of resources. This is the ideal guide for any leader who is committed to successful strategy execution."

— **Ron Kaufman**, Author, New York Times bestseller *Uplifting Service*

"Essential reading for anyone embarking on the strategy execution journey—Robin at his best."

— **Mel Carvill**, Director, Home Credit BV

"As expected from a pioneer and expert in the field of strategy implementation, it's chock-full of practical templates and tips that bring your strategy down to where it belongs—to your managers and employees who should execute it every day—and away from the consultants and board members who guide the organization. An easy read, not in the least because of Robin's quintessential use of humor and stories."

— **Bert van der Feltz**, CEO, East West Seed Group

"Robin Speculand is one of the few world thought leaders who understands the importance of project management to implement strategy successfully. His latest book, *Excellent in Execution*, is a masterpiece and a 'must have' for any executive."

— **Antonio Nieto-Rodriguez**, Duke CE Professor, World Champion in Project Management

"Robin continues to build effective tools leaders need to successfully implement organizational change and execute strategy. Our community should welcome these for impacting results.

"A great strategy is no guarantee of success. We need to also have that greater strategy for implementation and engagement. A solid plan of action and a sense of ownership and alignment to the new goals helps the new reality set in. With Robin's clarity of thinking and the resources provided in the book, we can get there from here."

— **Scott Simmerman**, PhD, CPF, CPT, Managing Partner, Performance Management Company

"In *Excellence in Execution*, Speculand brilliantly lays out a step-by-step guide to successfully execute on strategy. The checklists, toolkits and questions are a treasure trove for leaders. The DBS Bank case study brings the lessons to life. Highly recommended for leaders who want to leave their competitors in the dust."

— **Gina Carr**, Author, *Klout Matters*

"With the incredible speed at which every industry is moving in today's world, the potential to get distracted and derailed from implementation has never been greater. Leaders have a disproportionate impact on how teams get to action, so giving leaders a tool kit that will practically and rapidly help with implementation is not only helpful—it's vital."

— **Jean Kerr**, Change and Leadership "Geek," IT Industry

"Robin Speculand has done a marvelous job with his work, *Excellence in Execution*. I read this book in its entirely and was taking notes feverishly throughout. Speculand shows how the concept of strategy is not just about putting together nice ideas and resting. He shows how we need to see the implementation through to finish.

Even though it is not billed as a motivational book, I was strongly motivated to get moving in my own business. As I read what Speculand advised, I got ideas on how I could implement specific actions in my work. This book can inform and empower your team. Get it. Read it. Take action on it. Do this now before your competition gets their hands on it."

— **Terry Brock**, Author, Professional Speaker, Marketing Coach

"*Excellence in Execution* is built on a solid framework and tools for implementing strategy. This book is perfect for anyone responsible for or working on strategy implementation as it provides powerful execution guides that can be applied easily."

— **Professor Jochen Wirtz**, Vice-Dean Graduate Studies Director, UCLA, NUS Executive MBA, National University of Singapore

"It's a delight to read a practical book with personal examples from a seasoned implementer. *Excellence in Execution* systematically walks you through a well-thought-out blend of practical case studies, models, key tips, pointers and inspirational stories. It goes beyond what most books offer by explaining HOW to implement."

— **Andrew and Gaia Grant**, Directors of Tirian, Authors, *The Innovation Race*

EXCELLENCE
in
EXECUTION

HOW to Implement Your Strategy

Robin Speculand

NEW YORK

NASHVILLE • MELBOURNE • VANCOUVER

EXCELLENCE *in* EXECUTION
HOW to Implement Your Strategy

© 2017 **Robin Speculand**

Published in New York, New York, by Morgan James Publishing. Morgan James is a trademark of Morgan James, LLC. www.MorganJamesPublishing.com

The Morgan James Speakers Group can bring authors to your live event. For more information or to book an event visit The Morgan James Speakers Group at www.TheMorganJamesSpeakersGroup.com.

ISBN 978-1-68350-143-5 paperback
ISBN 978-1-68350-144-2 eBook
Library of Congress Control Number: 2016946878

In an effort to support local communities, raise awareness and funds, Morgan James Publishing donates a percentage of all book sales for the life of each book to Habitat for Humanity Peninsula and Greater Williamsburg.

Get involved today! Visit
www.MorganJamesBuilds.com

This book is dedicated to GraceKelly
who came into my life and swept my heart away.

Only when a strategy is successfully executed do you know if it was a good strategy.

Only when it's well executed do customers notice the difference.

Only when the execution succeeds does it positively impact shareholder value.

Table of Contents

Foreword

by Piyush Gupta

Robin continues his excellent work on strategy execution through his new book, Excellence in Execution. DBS is honored that he chose to use our own strategy execution journey as a case study in this book.

Robin's key point over the years has always resonated with me: creating the strategy is only half the battle, effective execution is the other half. In my own industry, I would argue that it is 20:80 ... what one needs to do is less impactful than actually getting it done!

DBS's journey during my tenure as CEO has had two distinct phases: Phase 1 (2010 – 2013) was about creating a world class multinational, Phase 2 (2014 to date) has been about creating a 20,000 people start-up. The strategic choices have evolved somewhat over the two phases. In the second period, we chose to double down on the strategies that brought us success, while course correcting in areas where we came up short. Perhaps most important, we have committed DBS unequivocally to a digital future and everything that entails: reimagining the customer journey, eliminating paper and designing for "no operations".

In both periods, our biggest challenge has been to get the organization moving and committed to our broad directions. I call this getting strategic alignment, perhaps a little bit deeper than what Robin refers to as "creating awareness". I find that while making a strategic choice is a question of weeks, getting alignment take much longer. Simple and memorable communication is an important part of this, as is the communication platform itself. An occasional (or even regular) email from the top will prove to be woefully inadequate. Town halls, workshops and two way dialogues are some tools that have helped. Most importantly, you need to create "ambassadors"... a body of front line leaders who will champion the message at various levels within the organization.

Setting the bar high, or committing to excellence, is a second big hurdle. Often this requires a dramatic shift in organization culture. In our own case, we needed to move from a somewhat bureaucratic culture to a more entrepreneurial and nimbler one. Creating such a culture change requires more than just preaching. We found that creating specific platforms for customer experience and innovation, and a process improvement methodology based on human centered design helped create a way for people to learn through doing. We had to ensure that people believed it was okay to take some risks, and that mistakes were acceptable if one learnt from them. A commitment to training (more than classrooms, we focused on exposure and experience) and internal mobility, accompanied by a robust talent identification and development program were key ingredients as well.

Having a rigorous business system with appropriate measures is the third piece in the puzzle. At DBS, we focused on creating appropriate Management Information Systems, and embraced the balanced scorecard approach, but made this a living tool. The scorecard is balanced across time (tactical versus strategic) as well as across stakeholders (shareholders versus others). It is agreed with the Board at the beginning of the year, and is cascaded down each operating unit. Individual KPIs are linked to the scorecard, so that there is clear line of sight between employee goals and organizational imperatives. There is a well-established rhythm towards performance monitoring, and rewards are closely linked to scorecard outcomes.

I do not wish to suggest that we have it all figured out… far from it. However, I do want to that suggest that our case study helps exemplify some of the practices that Robin has covered in this book so well. The greatest of strategies will fail if not executed well, and execution is a discipline that can be learnt.

Enjoy the book!

—**Piyush Gupta**, Chief Executive Officer, DBS Group

Introduction

Many people see execution as the toughest part of the strategy-execution equation. I see it as the most exciting and appealing part. Why? Because it's in the execution you realize the results, recognize the financial benefits and deliver on the strategy's phenomenal opportunities.

My personal mantra is "to transform the execution approach globally by changing leaders' attitude and approach." This passion has inspired me to write my fourth book on the subject, *Excellence in Execution–HOW to Implement Strategy*.

This book introduces the research, new thinking and methodology adopted by the clients of the consultancy I founded and operate, Bridges Business Consultancy Int. Bridges has been fortunate to work with clients that include Singapore Airlines, Cisco, Ikea, Estee Lauder, Visa, Honeywell, LVMH, Citigroup, Wipro, DBS Bank, Oracle, AXA, Ministry of Defense, UBS, Petronas, Home Credit, Microsoft, Aditya Birla, Jardines, MSIG, Standard Chartered, Philips, Informatica, UOB, Schneider Electric, B Braun, Autodesk, Maersk, East West Seed and many others.

My first book on implementation, *Bricks to Bridges–Make Your Strategy Come Alive* (published in 2004), has become an international bestseller. It explains why change management doesn't work when implementing strategy and why *execution* deserves to be a separate topic from *strategy* (which it was not at the time). *Bricks to Bridges* also introduces the Implementation Compass™—a framework for identifying the right actions to implement strategy.

In 2010, John Wiley & Sons published my follow-up book *Beyond Strategy– The Leader's Role in Successful Implementation,* also a bestseller. It was born out of feedback from leaders who said they learned from *Bricks to Bridges* what the *organization* had to do but not what *they* specifically had to do to lead the implementation.

In 2014, the eBook *The Pocket Book of Excellence in Execution–136 Key Messages for Your Success* was published. It assists leaders in understanding the execution challenge by providing tips, skills and best practices to adopt.

Now, *Excellence in Execution* provides you with the components you need to execute strategy well. It features 182 questions designed to create your organization's execution plan and 72 Powerful Execution Tips that are available as a separate eBook, *Building Your Execution Plan—182 Strategy Implementation Questions* and . . .

 12 Checklists of questions to ask and actions to take

 18 Toolkits you can readily adopt

Key chapters start with a QR Code access to a video that introduces the chapter's content and asks a provocative question. Please visit www. excellenceinexecutionbook.com/video to view all the videos.

 Scan this QR Code to see my introduction video to the book. (To download the scanner app go to www.scan.me/download).

The Implementation Hub (Hub)

This is the world's first portal to provide a singular link for finding a wealth of implementation knowledge. For access to download the toolkits, checklists and other material, visit www.implementation-hub.com/tools_tips_techniques/excellence-in-execution.

I created the Hub in 2013 as a central depository. It now features more than 500 tools, videos, templates, techniques, tips, best practices, media presentations, case studies, audits and other useful resources. This easy-to-access resource allows you to find what you need about implementation in one place. You'll save hours searching through endless websites, documents and blogs for material that supports your success. Specifically, you'll access supplementary information about strategy implementation including all the checklists and toolkits from *Excellence in Execution*.

Part One: Transforming the Approach

Part One of *Excellence in Execution* introduces opportunities for leaders to transform their approach to strategy execution. It explains the shift in thinking required to achieve Excellence in Execution. It also introduces new tools and language such as the Strategy Cadence, Execution Juxtaposition, Decoding the Execution Challenge, Mavericks Network, Review Rhythm and the Three Themes Broad of Execution, explained in depth in Part Two.

Part Two: Making It Your Own

The Three Broad Themes of Execution serve as the backbone for Part Two along with an in-depth case study on DBS Bank, one of the leading banks in Asia, and 182 designed questions for leaders to ask as they develop their execution plan.

The Three Broad Themes of Execution guide you through what needs to happen in your implementation journey to ultimately achieve Excellence in Execution. The themes are:

- Create Awareness
- Build Excellence
- Follow Through

DBS Bank has recognized the need for both a winning strategy and a successful execution. CEO Piyush Gupta and his leadership team kindly allowed me to interview team members, research the bank's approach and detail its successful five-year implementation journey for this book. A shorter version of the case study is available to purchase from Singapore Management University with teaching notes at http://casewriting.smu.edu.sg/case/dbs-bank-transformation-through-strategy-implementation.

At the end key each chapters in Part Two, you'll find thought-provoking questions to ask as you build your organization's execution plan. The HOW (How Organizations Win) echoes the book's subtitle through these questions.

Throughout both Part One and Part Two, you'll find Powerful Execution Tips, which are snippets of best practices. You can download a summary of these tips from the Implementation Hub at www.implementation-hub.com.

Excellence in Execution aims to transform your thinking about strategy execution and how you approach it. You won't always agree with everything you read, but that's my goal. I aim to provoke you into *thinking differently* and *taking different actions*—ones that can reverse the staggering failure rate of execution and assist in your organization's overall success.

I wish you all the best on your implementation journey. Please share with me your thoughts and experience as you apply what this book provides.

Robin Speculand
bridges@bridgesconsultancy.com
To receive daily implementation messages follow me on: https://www.linkedin.com/in/robinspeculand and
https://twitter.com/speculand and
https://www.facebook.com/BridgesBusinessConsultancy

How to use *Excellence in Execution* for maximum value

Author Profile

The current approach to implementing strategy it not working, and a different thinking is required.

Robin Speculand is driven to transform strategy implementation by inspiring leaders to change their attitude and approach. His work begins when leaders are crafting their organizations' strategy and starting to define how to implement it.

Robin is a global pioneer and expert in strategy implementation. He is the founder and CEO of Bridges Business Consultancy Int and creator of the Implementation Hub—the first portal in the world dedicated to strategy implementation featuring over 500 resources. Since assisting its first client, Singapore Airlines, Bridges has worked with governments, multinational corporations and local organizations across five continents to execute their strategies.

Guiding Bridge's clients' implementation journeys involves transferring knowledge, tools and templates developed over two decades. Tools Robin has innovated include the Implementation Compass™, a proprietary framework for successful implementation, IMPACT, a toolkit with a structured approach for implementing actions in 90 days and Readiness2Execute, an audit of your organization's execution capabilities.

A prolific writer and thinker on implementing strategy, Robin is an international bestselling author. His books include *Bricks to Bridges—Make Your Strategy Come Alive*, which set the benchmark for new thinking in his field, *Beyond Strategy—The Leader's Role in Successful Implementation*, John Wiley & Sons, *Building Your Execution Plan—182 Strategy Implementation Questions* and his latest, *Excellence in Execution—HOW to Implement Strategy*, Morgan James, that provides a new approach to adopting the right mindset, toolset and skillset.

His pioneering work has been featured on the BBC U.K. & Global, CNBC, Financial Times, Sunday Telegraph and Singapore Straits Times and in strategy journals and international print.

A sought-after keynote speaker at strategy and international business forums, Robin is also an award-winning case writer, an educator for Duke CE, the co-founder of the Strategy Implementation Institute, and an adjunct faculty member at the Office of Executive and Professional Education in Singapore Management University. Outside of work, he's a die-hard ironman athlete.

Robin Speculand is a global pioneer and expert in strategy implementation.

bridges@bridgesconsultancy.com
Bridges Business Consultancy Int Pte Ltd
+65 68860123

Part One

TRANSFORMING
THE APPROACH

——— *Chapter One* ———

Your Strategy on Trial

 Video Quiz: Is it better to take either no action or the wrong action when executing strategy, if you have to choose?

*A*s an essential business topic, strategy execution is in its infancy. Yet it's quickly evolving as leaders demand more knowledge, structure and resources on how to achieve it. When they address how to *execute* strategy, it's not always with the same energy, drive and conviction they applied to *crafting* it. Often, they are missing the skills and tools needed to excel in their execution efforts—a gap I aim to close with this book.

A leadership team doesn't walk into a conference room and declare, "Let's create a bad strategy!" Although they believe they have crafted a winning strategy by the end of the planning, *they only know if it's good once it's executed.*

Each step of your *implementation journey* (the words "implementation" and "execution" are used interchangeably and the term "implementation journey" carries your thinking forward) creates an opportunity to dramatically improve employee engagement, culture, performance and profits. Leaders can seize

3

this phenomenal opportunity by recognizing *why* execution has previously failed and *what* needs to happen differently to succeed. They can then lead the organization through the journey, delivering on strategy promises to customers and stakeholders along the way. By crafting a winning strategy and achieving Excellence in Execution, you have a powerful business differentiator over your competitors and the payoff is tremendous.

In addition, a well-led execution creates a positive environment, empowers people to improve the way they work, eliminates non-value-adding tasks, has specific measures and targets, and challenges obsolete procedures. It also encourages innovation as well as the right actions while regularly reinforcing and reviewing the strategy.

Once the execution begins, the theory starts to become the reality. The hard work of planning your organization's future comes into play as you test the thinking and assumptions. You discover how good (or bad) your strategy is. In effect, the strategy is being judged as if it's on trial.

> *Powerful Execution Tip:* After about six weeks, half the assumptions made on a strategic decision are forgotten. As we tend to forget assumptions, write them down and review them regularly to make sure they're still relevant.

When it's not the right strategy or it has been poorly executed, a negative cycle is set in motion that can lead to losing customers, top performers, revenue and market share.

The goal is for the leaders *and* people throughout the organization to understand HOW (How Organizations Win) to achieve Excellence in Execution so your strategy succeeds.

Why Focus on Excellence in Execution?

The 1950s-era criminal Willie Sutton was asked why he robbed banks. He allegedly replied, "That's where the money is." Similarly, why should leaders focus on Excellence in Execution? Because that's where the phenomenal opportunity is, as most organizations are still very poor at it.

Over the past decade, the latest research by Bridges[1] and others show an overall improvement in execution of strategy. (See Bridges' Research in Chapter Two.) Still, the current high failure rate demonstrates there's a long way to go. The methodologies, tools, techniques, templates, tips and other material available in this book assist you throughout your implementation journey.

Excellence in Execution assists leaders in achieving a greater than average revenue growth.

Execution is the Achilles Heel of Strategy

If too much emphasis is placed on strategy compared with execution, then it leads to lower levels of performance because leaders become occupied with *crafting* it rather than *executing* it. High performance comes from striking the right balance between crafting strategy and executing it for your organization.

A number of organizations have shifted their thinking from predominantly focusing on strategy to giving a balanced consideration to the strategy and its execution. This shift represents a "pendulum swing" in current thinking.

The Pendulum Swings

Over the past decade, the pendulum has swung from principally focusing on *crafting* strategy to *executing* it. (See Figure 1.1.)

Figure 1.1

---

1   http://www.implementation-hub.com/resources/implementation-surveys

Strategy planning was only introduced as a discipline in the mid-1960s, making it a relatively new topic in business. Since then, organizations are striving to develop their ability to craft strategy and we are still learning. For example, we understand the word "strategy," but we don't have a common global definition for it.

The catalyst for the pendulum swinging toward execution came from leaders realizing that strategies are failing more often than succeeding. It is, however, a slow-moving swing. If you search online, you'll find at least six times more search results for "strategy" than for "execution."

Which is more important—strategy or execution? This is a question being asked but it's truly a moot question, for both are equally important. It arose partly because leaders struggled to understand what was involved in this field of execution. As an example, Paul Leinwand, Cesare Mainardi and Art Kleiner stated in their 2015 *Harvard Business Review* article[2] that only 8% of leaders are effective at both creating good strategies and executing them.

Today, leaders appreciate it's not an either/or situation; it's both a strategy *and* execution priority. The question becomes HOW to achieve Excellence in Execution?

Lloyd Blankfein, the CEO and chairman of Goldman Sachs, stated, "For a company in Goldman's position, the response to current tough conditions is not wholesale strategic change, but rather one of tactical execution. For us, good strategy is effective execution."

In its report *Why Good Strategies Fail*, the Economist Intelligence Unit reported in "Lessons for the C-Suite"[3] that senior executives recognize the importance of strategy implementation. Yet a majority of executives admit their companies fall short. They acknowledge a disconnect between strategy formulation and implementation.

As we are in the initial stages of discovering what it takes to achieve Excellence in Execution, today's business pendulum is swinging *toward*

---

2   https://hbr.org/2015/12/only-8-of-leaders-are-good-at-both-strategy-and-execution
3   http://www.pmi.org/~/media/PDF/Publications/WhyGoodStrategiesFail_Report_EIU_
      PMI.ashx

execution. That means more force is required to gain movement, especially as the skills for strategy execution are new to many leaders. In the next few years, the pendulum will find an equilibrium position with equal force on strategy and execution. It will, however, take a global transformation in the approach to create the right balance.

Powerful Execution Tip: If your strategy does not provide a competitive advantage, then Excellence in Execution needs to provide it.

Part of the leaders' challenge is to strike the right balance between *crafting* the strategy and *executing* it for their organization.

One organization that has found the right balance is IKEA. It has a winning strategy that can be described as Excellence in Execution.

The organization's business model is to provide DIY furniture at good value. It minimizes shipping costs by packaging products tightly rather than in large rectangular boxes that create a high volume of wasted space. Assembly work once done by the retailer is pushed to the consumer, allowing IKEA to offer greater value for the money spent.

Its straightforward model is easy to understand and replicate, but who competes with IKEA across continents? IKEA has no direct global competitors because, even though its business model is well understood, no one can compete with its Excellence in Execution. That staves off competition and gives IKEA a competitive advantage.

The IKEA organization is fanatical about doing its own research, paying attention to detail, taking the right actions and offering customers the best value. Part of its success is the organization's slow execution speed to allow attention for detail. For example, its leaders take six years before entering a new market to ensure they understand the country's culture and can design their store accordingly.

This attention to detail also partly stems from the mistakes made when IKEA entered the U.S. market in the mid-1980s. IKEA rushed in without doing enough due diligence. Although this unprecedented way to shop for furniture quickly became a success, it was not without its growing pains, and IKEA paid the price for not understanding the American culture. For example, its bedding was the wrong size for U.S. beds. Also, the company sold flowerpots that Americans bought and used as water jugs!

Today, IKEA leverages its volume sales to predominantly middle-class consumers. Its people have become skilled at showing how the same products fit into different cultures. One of its Billy bookcases, for example, is sold every 10 seconds somewhere in the world.

In the next few years, the pendulum will swing back from focusing more on execution and then settle equally between strategy and execution. The next chapter examines the current state of execution in organizations around the world based on Bridges' research.

---- *Chapter Two* ----

What's Going On?

Video Quiz: What percentage of executions succeed?

*I*n 2002, Bridges Business Consultancy Int (Bridges) published its first research, http://www.implementation-hub.com/resources/implementation-surveys, citing that nine out of 10 strategy implementations fail, where we measure success as achieving at least 50% of the strategy objectives in the time allocated. These results became a wakeup call for leaders. (Note: In the initial survey, we had to replace the term "implementation" with "change" as "implementation" was not yet part of the business language in 2002.)

Bridges regularly conducts research to identify the state of execution and understand the challenges leaders are facing. In 2016, for our latest research, we interviewed 143 leaders. Of these, 28% were CEOs or board members and 63% were organizational leaders. The remainder came from other parts of the organization. The majority of the organizations were multinational corporations with annual revenues of more than US$50,000,000 a year. They came from a variety of industries including banking and finance, technology, consultancy and government.

The Good News: Research Shows Improvement

Over the 15 years Bridges has been conducting its research, strategy execution has improved by 23% from 90% in 2002 (our first research) to 67% in 2016. In 2005, Kaplan and Norton[4] echoed the 90% result. Neilson, Martin and Powers[5] published in 2008 that the rate was 60%. *The Economist*[6] published in 2013 that 61% were failing and McKinsey[7] reported the number in 2015 at 70%.

The good news? This is an improvement. The bad news? The odds are still stacked against your implementation success, making it more likely your organization will fail than succeed. (See Figure 2.1.)

Figure 2.1

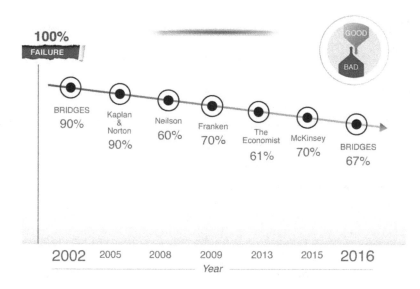

---

4   http://www.hbs.edu/faculty/Publication%20Files/05-071.pdf
5   https://hbr.org/2008/06/the-secrets-to-successful-strategy-execution
6   http://www.pmi.org/~/media/PDF/Publications/WhyGoodStrategiesFail_Report_EIU_PMI.ashx
7   http://www.mckinsey.com/insights/leading_in_the_21st_century/changing_change_management

Overview of Bridges' 2016 Results

According to survey results over 15 years, the most common corporate-wide initiatives to be implemented are:

1. Vision, mission and values
2. Crafting a new corporate strategy
3. Digital mindset

Interestingly, respondents have less belief that their organization is good at developing strategy than they did in 2012 (result is down from 80% to 68%) while their belief that their organization is good at implementing strategy has been virtually identical over the four years (46% "yes" and 54% "no"). Potentially contributing to this is almost half of the organizations (49%) spend less than 10 hours a month discussing the strategy as opposed to operations and day-to-day challenges. The marginally good news is that this marks an improvement from the 70% in 2012.

Almost half (48%) of the respondents see implementation equal in importance to strategy in their organization, while 34% view implementation as more important than strategy and only 18% view strategy as more important than implementation. Two-thirds (68%) say the organization has the leadership talent required to successfully implement the strategy, yet almost one third (32%) of respondents rate their organization as "poor" or "very poor" in its ability to implement.

The top three reasons for implementation failing has changed from 2012. Currently, they are:

1. Poor communication
2. Lack of leadership
3. Using the wrong measures

In 2012, the results were:

1. Not ensuring people are taking the right actions
2. Aligning implementation to the culture
3. Gaining people's support

In addition, 78% of respondents say their immediate boss shows recognition for their implementation contribution, and 43% say their organization has an effective measurement system such as the Balanced Scorecard for tracking measures.

A new question in the 2016 survey was, "How often do you review the implementation for the whole organization?" Results showed 43% review it only once or twice a year while 20% review it monthly.

The key takeaways from Bridges' latest research are:

- The failure rate is still too high and a new approach and way of thinking is required.
- Businesses are improving their ability to execute.
- Leaders spend less than 10 hours a month discussing the strategy, which is not enough.
- The reasons execution is failing constantly fluctuate depending on organizational circumstances.
- Fewer leaders believe their organization is good at developing strategy in 2016 compared with 2012.
- One third of leaders rate their organization "poor" or "very poor" in its ability to implement.
- One in every two leaders rates execution equal in emphasis to strategy.
- Two thirds of leaders believe their organization has the talent to achieve Excellence in Execution, but one third rate their organization "poor" or "very poor" at it.
- Only one in five organizations reviews its execution monthly.

Challenging Conventional Thinking

Leaders have a responsibility to craft and execute a winning strategy—one that ensures the organization's future. Success, though, often requires leaders to challenge conventional thinking. Consider these points:

- It's better to have Excellence in Execution than a winning strategy because you then *know* how good or bad the strategy is. From there, you can make adjustments as required during the execution phase.
- Good execution can mitigate poor strategy but not vice versa.
- It's better to take the wrong action than no action at all to generate meaningful traction. *Note: This is the answer to the video question at the start of this chapter.*

When an organization is taking the wrong actions, it is at least in motion and not stagnant. Then when it corrects itself, it becomes easier to take the right actions as it is already in the habit of taking action.

The Tremendous Payoff

When you challenge conventional thinking and achieve Excellence in Execution, the financial rewards await you. When you don't, your organization can pay a heavy price through decreasing cash flow and profits. Consider these facts:

- On average, companies deliver only 63% of the financial performance their strategies promise, based on research by Michael C. Mankins and Richard Steele.[8]
- Failing at strategy implementation can cost up to 50% of an organization's potential cumulative cash flow, according to CEB, a best practice insight and technology company.[9]
- Poor performance results in organizations losing $109 million for every $1 billion invested in projects and programs and only 9% of organizations rate themselves excellent in execution, according to Project Management Institute (PMI) research.[10]

---

8   https://hbr.org/2005/07/turning-great-strategy-into-great-performance
9   http://www.multivu.com/players/English/7082252-ceb-executive-guidance-for-2015-closing-strategy-to-execution-gaps/
10 https://www.pmi.org/-/media/PDF/Business-Solutions/PMI_Pulse_2014.ashx

By comparison, consider these results:

- When senior leaders are aligned—a benefit of being Excellent in Execution—CEB estimates a 39% better return on growth investments.[11]
- Organizations with high employee engagement—a benefit of being Excellent in Execution—had a 19% increase in operating income and a 28% growth in earnings per share, according to research by Towers Watson[12] of 50 organizations over a one-year period.
- "Every company 'leaks' value at various stages of the implementation process," stated McKinsey & Company researchers. They also said, that "good-implementer respondents say their companies sustained twice the value from their prioritized opportunities two years after the change efforts ended, compared with those at poor implementers."[13]
- Mankins and Steele[14] also state that if leaders were to realize the full potential of the organization's current strategy, the increase in value could be as much as 60% to 100%!

Achieving Excellence in Execution often requires a shift in the leaders' and organization's philosophy.

The Excellence in Execution Philosophy

Donald Sull, Rebecca Homkes and Charles Sull in their article "Why Strategy Execution Unravels—and What to Do About It" in *Harvard Business Review, March 2015,* made this observation: "If common beliefs about execution are incomplete at best and dangerous at worst, what should take their place? The starting point is a fundamental redefinition of execution as the ability to seize

---

11   http://www.executiveboard.com/exbd-resources/pdf/executive-guidance/eg2015-annual-final.pdf?cn=pdf

12   http://chiefexecutive.net/how-employee-engagement-drives-business-success/

13   http://www.mckinsey.com/insights/operations/why_implementation_matters

14   https://hbr.org/2005/07/turning-great-strategy-into-great-performance

opportunities aligned with the strategy while coordinating with other parts of the organization on an ongoing basis."[15]

Achieving Excellence in Execution requires a different philosophy than many leaders currently have. The Excellence in Execution philosophy from an organization's perspective and compiled since 2000 is summarized in Figure 2.2. Figure 2.3 summarizes it from a leader's perspective.

Organization's Perspective Figure 2.2

Current Philosophy	*Excellence in Execution Philosophy*
1. Past mistakes The organization doesn't learn from past mistakes and, even worse, leaders keep repeating them. If there's any improvement, it's typically incremental.	**Become a learning organization** The organization asks, "What went wrong in past executions?" before starting the next and ensures it learns from the error of its ways. Along with quantum leaps in improvement, this is what's needed to be Excellent in Execution.
2. Poor execution planning Most of the planning time is spent crafting the strategy and only a little on preparing the execution. Naturally, leaders think their new strategy is good, but the only way to know if it's good or bad is by executing it.	**Execution is part of the strategy** Planning the execution has the same importance as crafting a winning strategy. The execution plan is in place before launching the strategy. The time taken to prepare for strategy execution is not taken from crafting the strategy; it's added on to the timeline. This is time well invested.
3. Strategy a mile wide and an inch deep The launch of a new strategy causes confusion in any organization. This is added to when individual leaders perceive the strategy differently. Leaders understand the impact of the strategy across the business (a mile wide) but not the implications on the vertical business (a mile deep). They also see the strategy from their own perspective and communicate it to their people from that perspective. This leads to inconsistent messages and even greater confusion.	**Strategy a mile wide and a mile deep** Before launching the strategy to the whole organization, ensure the leaders know the expected result on their business lines and have an overview of the strategy's impact across the organization. This creates greater alignment in communications, reduces confusion and drives the right actions.

---

15   https://hbr.org/2015/03/why-strategy-execution-unravelsand-what-to-do-about-it

Current Philosophy	*Excellence in Execution Philosophy*

4. Wrong measures are used
Leaders plan their new strategy and then launch it but fail to change the organization's measures. They are trying to execute the new strategy while measuring old ones. As a result, they fail because people do what leaders *measure*, more than what they *say*.

Change your strategy, change your measures
"What gets measured gets done" is as true today as it was when it was first said. At a time when analytics are growing exponentially, it is more critical than ever to ensure you have the right measures in place to drive the right actions. Identify the measures that track your strategy objectives.

5. Strategy requires a long-term
perspective, yet leaders run the business with a short-term view
When leaders are held accountable for short-term performance, they deliver short-term results, even when that approach is detrimental to the strategy. Being driven by quarterly performance often conflicts with the required long-term strategic actions.

Managing the strategic juxtaposition
Leaders have to focus on both short-term and long-term business performance. For this to happen, they work in an environment that not only encourages this balance but supports it through the systems and structure. For example, they set up rewards for both quarterly and long-term results.

6. Execution never goes according to plan
Whatever was planned in the boardroom will change in the execution. Although few absolutes exist in business, this is one. As people take action to execute the strategy, variables fluctuate, such as customers' expectations, markets and people. Yet leaders often fail to adjust the execution plan accordingly.

Agility in execution
It is essential to regularly review the execution and adjust it as required to overcome changing circumstances. Leaders have to reflect on what's happening and become agile around the execution to make the necessary changes.

7. No follow up occurs
In organizations, a key reason people don't follow through on their intentions is because they're not held accountable for their actions.

Take the right actions
If you want to become fit, you have to train. If you want a degree, you have to study. If you want to be promoted, you have to excel. All these require one constant: the right actions. To execute a goal, you must believe in it, commit to it and act on it. These three components are consistently required and especially when executing strategy. People must also know their immediate boss will check on their performance by tracking and measuring it.

Current Philosophy	Excellence in Execution Philosophy
8. Culture does not support the execution	**Culture drives the way you implement**
The culture of an organization is dictated by many things such as behaviors, expectations, stories and heroes. When there is misalignment between the culture of the organization and the essence of the strategy, then it fails to be executed.	Every organization's culture is different; therefore, every execution is unique. That's why leaders need to identify how the culture drives the execution and make the execution their own.

Leader's Perspective Figure 2.3

Current Philosophy	Excellence in Execution Philosophy
1. Top-heavy strategy	**Balanced approach**
Time is spent thinking through the impact of the strategy at the top of the organization. Corporate-wide objectives and goals are identified from the top down, as is communication. After leaders spend months (and sometimes years) discussing a new strategy, they then take a short time to explain it to the rest of the organization. Within a brief time, people are expected to understand why there is a new strategy and how to execute it. And they're expected to feel inspired to do so.	During the execution, leaders need to devote at least the same time and energy they spent crafting the plan on driving and guiding the execution. They become the "Voice of the Strategy," leveraging every opportunity to talk about it, share it and explain it. Beyond the town-hall meeting, they address their people at team meetings, off-sites, one-on-ones, workshops, etc. They also give their people time to understand why a new strategy is essential to the business and what it means to them. They also answer question on how they can participate.
2. Not clear on how to implement	**Guide your people to take the right actions**
Even when people are willing to participate in the rollout of the new strategy and are inspired to do so, they struggle. Why? Leaders don't identify the right actions to take. Strategy is viewed from 50,000 feet up, but its execution happens at the ground level. The people on the ground toil to translate the lofty strategy into their day-to-day work.	Leaders are responsible for translating the "big picture" into people's everyday work so they can identify and take the right actions. They create the context and environment that inspires employees to want to participate in the execution and guides them to know what to do.

Current Philosophy	*Excellence in Execution Philosophy*
3. Leaders underestimate the execution challenge Leaders habitually underestimate the challenge of executing strategy. By doing so, they don't allocate the required resources such as budget, people and time. Therefore, before the strategy is even launched, it is set up to fail!	**Execution is more complicated than most leaders think** The only way to know if you have a winning strategy is to successfully execute it. Leaders take the time to understand the challenges and prepare the execution landscape with the required resources to set up people for success.
4. Not my job to execute Being invited to assist in carving out the future of the organization by crafting the new strategy is exciting. Execution isn't regarded with the same excitement. Leaders thus delegate the responsibility of championing the execution. But when they take their attention off the execution, so do their people. Crafting the strategy does not mean the execution is a fait accompli.	**Stay personally engaged** Leaders are responsible for crafting the strategy and driving and guiding its execution. They must personally stay engaged and committed throughout the whole implementation journey.
5. Overload of objectives When people have to deal with too many objectives, they can become paralyzed. They don't know where to start and what to do. As a result, they end up doing little, if anything, around the execution.	**Less is more** You have more chance of achieving Excellence in Execution if you focus on fewer objectives. The more you try to do, the less you actually accomplish. It's better to focus on fewer actions.
6. Communication poor and inadequate As communication becomes easier through mobile devices, blogs, social media, etc., leaders become poorer at communicating their strategy. Many people in an organization—even as high as 95%—can't tell you their own organization strategy. If they don't know what it is, they can never execute it. After leaders announce the new strategy, they do little communication beyond that.	**Communication is effective** This involves providing constant communication throughout the whole implementation journey. After the initial launch, the organization continues to communicate, for example, what lessons are being learned, what is happening, what is coming next. As well as sharing best practices feedback from different stakeholders on an on-going basis and updates against progress against the strategy objectives.

Current Philosophy	*Excellence in Execution Philosophy*
7. No support given by bosses People are willing to step up and take risks to support the new strategy. Yet, when they do, often they receive no encouragement or support from their immediate bosses. As a result, they stop taking the new actions, and the execution falters.	**Positive reinforcement given regularly** Leaders must not only task their people to identify the right actions and inspire them to take them; they must also support the right actions by giving positive and regular reinforcement.

The reasons for execution failures are numerous because the challenges are unique to each organization and leader. That's why each organization and leader should examine their own execution capabilities. Chapter Five introduces how this can be achieved using the Readiness2Execute Assessment.

That said, some proven Excellence in Execution principles and techniques are common among successful executions. Once leaders identify which reasons for failing relate to their organization and themselves, they can then make their execution their own by adopting the appropriate ones.

 What is the Philosophy in *Your* Organization?

Take a moment to reflect on your leadership and your organization's philosophy. Then determine what you can do differently by rating yourself and your organizational philosophy templates.

Organization's and Leader's perspective philosophy templates are available at www.implementation-hub.com/tools_tips_techniques/excellence-in-execution along with all the other toolkits, checklists and other material.

Leaders have the role of assisting people in thinking—and acting—differently because, in Excellence in Execution, leaders don't execute the strategy. Their people do.

The next chapter further clarifies a leader's role in achieving Excellence in Execution.

Chapter Three

A Leader's Role in Achieving Excellence in Execution

 Video Quiz: What percentage of leaders believes their organization's strategy will lead to success?

To guide their organizations through the implementation journey, leaders are responsible for crafting a winning strategy and then involving and leading the rest of the organization in its execution. Leaders coach their people, step in to resolve issues and ensure the right outcomes are being achieved. As they champion the big-picture direction the organization is heading, they guide people accordingly and drive the execution. The challenge is achieving this.

Failure is Constantly Watching

Before you even start your implementation journey, the odds are stacked against you as more executions fail than succeed. Many leaders are guilty of delegating the execution and not paying adequate attention to it. When they do this, their people also stop paying attention to it. McKinsey & Company stated that "Half of all efforts to transform organization performance fail either because leaders don't act as role models for change or because people in the organization defend the status quo."[16]

> *Powerful Execution Tip*: If leaders perceive execution as an *interruption* to the business, they will not drive and champion it.

Anything short of embracing a new strategy and its execution by leaders can be seen by employees as a lack of confidence in the strategy itself. That feeling will spread throughout the organization.

- If you only apply lip service to the execution without championing it, employees will sense the lack of commitment and not step up; the execution will fail.
- If you don't create the time to oversee the implementation journey, explain why the organization needs to transform, and change the agenda then employees will sense the lack of commitment and not step up; the execution will fail.
- If you don't set the strategy and create the budget to allocate required funding, employees will sense the lack of commitment and not step up; the execution will fail.

A key question to consider is: "What are you willing to do to execute your organization's strategy?"

In contrast, execution progresses when leaders support their comments with actions. Because only so much can go on a leader's radar, he or she has to carefully select which actions will best drive the execution forward and where to invest time.

---

16 http://www.mckinsey.com/global-themes/leadership/change-leader-change-thyself

Powerful Execution Tip: Cut in half your current projects, measures and objectives so you can focus on what's really important.

Booz & Company (now called Strategy&)[17] surveyed executives from around the world on the results of their organizations' strategic initiatives. Given more than 2,350 responses, the findings suggest a high degree of disillusionment, including:

- Two-thirds (67%) say their company's capabilities do not fully support the company's own strategy and the way it creates value in the market.
- Only one in five executives (21%) thinks the company has a "right to win" in all the markets it competes in.
- Most of the respondents (53%) don't believe their company's strategy would lead to success. *This is the answer to the video question.*

If leaders don't believe in the strategy, they will never be authentic and sincere in executing it.

A significant shift in strategy requires a significant change in a leader's day-to-day activities across the organization.

Powerful Execution Tip: In every organization there are actions detrimental to the strategy execution. It is critical to identify and eliminate them.

A significant shift in strategy requires a significant change in resource allocation across the organization.

---

17   https://hbr.org/2011/06/making-your-strategy-more-relevant

Need for Authenticity and Sincerity

When leaders create the right conditions for execution and guide people through the journey, it demonstrates their authentic commitment and sincerity. If they try to fake it, their people will pick up on it and turn their backs on the execution. McKinsey & Company stated that "Leaders see their role and personal fulfillment wrapped up in setting a strategy, but don't have the same level of commitment and sense of reward and responsibility in implementing it. It's normally perceived as 'down a level.' Leaders need to reframe how they perceive implementation and its importance and their personal role and responsibility in making sure it is planned for and happens! Research indicates that if companies can identify and address pervasive mindsets at the outset, they are four times more likely to succeed in an organizational-change effort than are companies that overlook this stage."[18]

A challenge occurs when not all the leaders in the organization demonstrate commitment and sincerity. In fact, many demonstrate the opposite, which can sabotage the execution. This is when the CEO must make crucial decisions and, if necessary, adjust the strategy by changing the leaders. For example, both Jack Welch and John Chambers recognized this early on when they launched their new strategy at GE and Cisco respectively. They took the corrective action of dismissing leaders whom they believed did not make the mark.

Under the stewardship of former Group CEO Wolfgang Baler, Singapore Post had also been on a transformational journey to integrate ecommerce logistics with its traditional postal service. When Baler joined Singapore Post in 2011, he observed that many of the established leaders couldn't take the organization forward as they lacked the right mindset. He changed more than two-thirds of the leadership team, saying, "The key to a successful leader in transformations today is that he needs to understand the digital space, has the right courage and entrepreneurial approach but also can manage the P&L successfully." Such a dramatic change of the leadership team sends ripples throughout the organization, conveying that no matter

---

18   http://www.mckinsey.com/business-functions/organization/our-insights/the-irrational-side-of-change-management

where you sit, if you're not up to making the new strategy work, then you are out.

In another example, Angela Ahrendts became CEO of Burberry in 2006 (she later joined Apple). At her first strategy meeting on a cold rainy day with her top 60 leaders, she observed that not one of them was wearing a Burberry trench coat. Her leaders clearly weren't leading by example. Where was the authentic commitment and sincerity when they weren't even wearing their own rain coats on a rainy day?

In a similar example, on the first day when Alan Mulally joined Ford in 2006 as the new CEO, he drove into the executive car park and noticed his executives were not driving Ford cars! If the leaders don't drive their own product, then how can they lead by example to execute a strategy?

Powerful Execution Tip: A nod of an executive's head in a strategy meeting does not indicate an authentic and sincere commitment.

 Leading with Authenticity and Sincerity

Are you prepared to:

- ✓ Drive and champion the organization in the right direction?
- ✓ Model whatever is required?
- ✓ Inspire and guide your people?
- ✓ Constantly clarify what to focus on (and what not to focus on) for your people?
- ✓ Offer *employability*—learning in addition to work and pay?
- ✓ Ensure the right resources are available?
- ✓ Coach people to take the right actions?
- ✓ Empower people to take the right actions?
- ✓ Hold people accountable for taking the right actions?
- ✓ Encourage superior performance?

✓ Build a network that allows teams to communicate and be self-sufficient?

✓ Constantly review performance?

✓ Provide feedback on what's working and what's not?

Commit the Time and Energy

Even though leaders instinctively know execution requires extra effort, few are able to free up valuable time and resources to do it justice. Some are not willing and others are basically hoping it won't be needed. As a result, little energy toward the execution is displayed. Committing the time for execution every week in your schedule is a best practice. It also shows authentic commitment and sincerity.

As a leader, when you reallocate your personal time and focus, you send a powerful message across the whole organization. If you don't commit the time yourself, how can you expect others to? And if people don't see your energy in a visible way especially at the start of the journey, then they will question the organization's commitment to strategy execution.

**Carve out time and energy to *transform*
the business rather than only *run* it.**

It's estimated that 67% of a leader's time is spent making or receiving reports. If this percentage seems accurate for you, then it begs the following questions (not just for reports alone but for managing your time daily).

 Ways to Carve Out Time and Energy to Transform the Business

✓ If the report was not sent out for six months, would you miss it?

✓ Do you really need to attend every meeting on your agenda?

✓ Could you send your number two person instead of attending personally?

✓ What could you be doing that is more productive than the meeting?

✓   Is the agenda for the meeting the *right* agenda?

✓   Is there a better format you could be asking your team to use? For example, could you do a one-page or 20-minute summary of the essential information?

✓   Do you do the work you *want* to do or the work you *should* do?

> *Powerful Execution Tip*: An important part of a leader's time is spent being more visible in the organization during the implementation journey.

How to Influence Your People

Dr. Robert Cialdini, professor of psychology and marketing at Arizona State University, provides interesting research[19] in the area of influencing people. He has developed six universal principles of persuasion to influence people on taking the right actions. In the list that follows, I have taken his points and linked them to achieving Excellence in Execution.

1.   Reciprocity—People say yes when they owe you a favor especially that was personal and unexpected. This is as simple as tasting a new cheese on a stick and then when giving back the stick, we feel obligated to at least listen to them.

    To achieve Excellence in Execution, do small favors for others such as staying late to assist them. They will feel an obligation to assist you when you might need it.

2.   Scarcity—When something is exclusive and limited we want it more. One organization built a library and found that it had very little usage. Access was then changed to a privilege for only top performers and demand for access went up.

    To achieve Excellence in Execution, explain what is unique about the strategy and create an exclusive group to participate with the top leaders from the most talented employees.

---

19   http://www.influenceatwork.com/

3. Authority—People follow leaders they trust. You build trust by doing what you said you were going to do. For example, Dr. Cialdini conducted a study in which hospital physical therapists were asked to display all their awards and credentials. Compliance went up 30% immediately.

   To achieve Excellence in Execution, follow through on your commitments and support your people when required.

4. Consistency—Gain a small commitment first; for example, start with easy and quick actions and ask people to volunteer.

   To achieve Excellence in Execution, ask employees first if they will participate in the execution and more people will take the right actions.

5. Liking—Exchange personal information and find areas of similarity; people say yes to people they feel similar to. We assign more credibility and knowledge to people who speak slightly more rapidly, with the emphasis on slightly. Speaking too fast can make you appear insincere.

   To achieve Excellence in Execution, leaders need to get to know their people and pay them sincere compliments while speaking slightly more rapidly.

6. Consensus—Point out what others are already doing; people want to do what their peers are doing well. In an experiment, Dr. Cialdini influenced the behavior of hotel guests using towels by changing the card in the bathroom. Instead of the card saying "think of the environment," it was changed to "the majority of guests who stay at our hotel recycle their towels at least once." This true statement increased compliance by 28%.

   To achieve Excellence in Execution, find others whose behavior is desired and share what they are doing as role models.[20]

Another powerful way to influence people and their actions is to make sure they're working on essential projects that add value to the new strategy and desired outcomes.

Aligning Projects to Add Value

At the start of your implementation journey, a powerful way to demonstrate what has to be transformed is to review the *value* of the current projects against the new strategic objectives.

---

20   For more, watch https://www.youtube.com/watch?v=cFdCzN7RYbw

Powerful Execution Tip: To know where an organization is heading, look at its current projects and see how well they align. A lack of alignment undermines an organization's agility.

I was working with one organization whose technology team was about to purchase software that, under the organization's new direction, no longer had value. The leaders questioning this caught the discrepancy using the Alignment Exercise. They saved hundreds of thousands of dollars and time by putting a stop to the purchase and more importantly they were able to allocate funding and time to the right actions.

The Alignment Exercise provides an opportunity to review what is currently keeping people busy and making sure the work adds value to the new strategy. It also allows you to glance at current initiatives, see their alignment to the new strategy objectives, reduce the number of projects going on and eliminate the non-value-adding activities.

 Alignment Exercise

This exercise involves the following steps:

1. Hang flipchart paper that has swim lanes. (To create swim lanes, fold a piece of flipchart paper in half, then half again then half again and open it up.)
2. On the horizontal plane, list the new strategy objectives for the whole organization in separate lanes. (This can also be conducted at the departmental level.)
3. Identify and agree on the major initiatives currently underway. A major initiative is one that affects the old or new strategy and is visible at the C-Suite level. If you question whether an initiative should be included, err on the side of caution and include it.
4. On the vertical plane, list all the major initiatives in the lanes.

5. Review the initiative against the new strategy objectives and place a tick in the lane that adds value to the objectives of the new strategy.
6. Review any initiative that does not have any ticks and decide if it should continue or be stopped.
7. Review the boxes with ticks and prioritize them against the new strategy objectives.

By doing this exercise, you eliminate the initiatives that no longer add value to the business. This also frees up time and resources to take the right actions that *do* add value.

Powerful Execution Tip: To demonstrate the importance of a project and its value, link its successful completion to people's bonuses. The more important the project, the higher the percentage of bonus.

It's critical to select the right actions; they directly affect the market value of the organization.

Chapter Four presents why execution is part of strategy planning and introduces the HOW—the course of actions. You'll find out why change management doesn't decode the execution of strategy. You'll also note why *implementation never goes according to plan.*

—— *Chapter Four* ——

Decoding the Execution Challenge

 Video Quiz: Should you wait to complete the strategy before starting to execute it?

*F*or organizations to succeed, achieving Excellence in Execution requires the implementation planning to be part of the strategy planning.

Good Strategy Includes the Execution Plan

During the strategy planning, leaders must identify what needs to be executed so they can guide the organization through the implementation journey.

It's better to postpone your strategy launch until you have an execution plan than launch it without having your plan in place.

Leaders often focus more on *crafting* the strategy than *executing* it and exclude necessary details. Without a detailed plan in place, leaders can struggle

30

with what to do first after the strategy launch. Where should they allocate resources? Should they focus on communicating the new strategy? Do they need to provide the new skills training? Should they put in place new measures? The uncertainty in being unable to answer these frequent questions breeds confusion, discontent and lack of confidence. That in turn undermines any opportunity for the new strategy to gain traction.

Figure 4.1 shows the current approach. Compare it with the Excellence in Execution approach in Figure 4.2.

Figure 4.1: Current Approach

Figure 4.2: Excellence in Execution Approach

In Excellence in Execution, execution is planned as part of the organization's strategy planning and prepared before it's launched.

Shifting between the two approaches can make the difference between success and failure when leaders take the time to develop the HOW (How Organizations Win) in a detailed and rigorous way. The HOW ensures a smart start. It guides you through the implementation journey by allocating required resources, providing direction and maintaining momentum. It also assists in demonstrating the leaders' authentic commitment and sincerity.

Powerful Execution Tip: If leaders regard strategy execution as a standalone project, it will fail.

Leaders demonstrate an appreciation of execution by moving the execution planning into the strategy planning.

After crafting the strategy, ensure the CEO spends time with all business heads to ensure their business strategy is aligned to the corporate strategy.

Powerful Execution Tip: If leaders argue against taking time to discuss the execution during the planning because they do not see the value, then the probability of success is low.

Taking time to develop your execution plan doesn't dilute from the strategy planning. Rather, it adds tremendous long-term value. Having an enriched conversation among those in leadership results in:

- Further defining the strategy to all the leaders
- Stating what needs to be done in more detail to achieve Excellence in Execution
- Detailing the expected timeline of execution
- Clearly articulating the strategy outcomes
- Specifying individual responsibilities
- Starting the implementation journey with the right resources and capabilities
- Building belief and confidence across the organization

A good strategy well executed transforms the experience from doing challenging, confusing and complicated tasks to being engaging, enjoyable and even exhilarating. It decodes the tough challenge of execution to give everyone focus while dramatically increasing the odds for success. This is especially true when the execution is developed with the same intensity and energy as the strategy itself.

Powerful Execution Tip: By preparing a detailed HOW plan you set people up for success.

Reflect on how detailed your past execution plans have been compared to the strategy. If there is a significant difference, then it's likely the execution has not been thought through adequately.

Why Change Management Doesn't Decode the Execution Challenge

Change management has frequently been the default approach for executing strategy. It works well for projects and initiatives within departments and divisions but not for the corporate-wide execution of a strategy. If it did, there wouldn't be such a high failure rate.

I have been ardently arguing against using change management to execute strategy since 2000 when I started researching why it fails.

Change management is a *component* of strategy execution and shouldn't be used for executing it.

The approach for adopting change management is often linear—that is, the leadership team crafts a plan, shares it top-down, appoints champions, engages the whole organization, celebrates success and so on. By comparison, Excellence in Execution is not linear; you don't follow a one-to-ten list.

Change management also doesn't work for execution because achieving Excellence in Execution requires transformation from the core. Figure 4.3 on the next page provides an illustration of that.

Change management typically involves only change around the core. Transformation has to come from the heart of the business, not peripheral change.

Decoding the execution challenge requires that leaders of each organization *make it their own*.

Figure 4.3

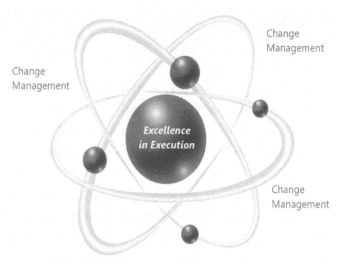

In addition, leaders need to identify the starting and ending points and what needs to happen in between—a journey that's unique for every organization.

Once you have the core principles of the strategy in place—about 80%, including the execution plan— that's when you start on your implementation journey. *This is the answer to this chapter's video question.*

Leaders sometimes strive to complete the strategy before they start the execution. This is a mistake as there's no such thing as a complete strategy due to constant change and accelerating pace of business. Both internal and external forces keep affecting the strategy and it needs to remain fluid.

Strategy is predominantly designed from the outside in—that is, you evaluate the external market then look inside. As Sun Tzu wrote in *The Art of War,* "Know your enemy, know yourself."[21] Why must you know the strength of your enemy first? By knowing the strength of your "enemy"—your competitors—you know where you stand against them.

---

21   Sun Tzu. The Art of War. Filiquarian. 2007.

Execution is principally designed from the inside out—that is, you assess your internal capabilities and determine what needs to transform. Therefore, once you have about 80% of the strategy complete, it's time to start executing it. Then you adjust as required throughout the journey.

> *Powerful Execution Tip*: Execution progresses when leaders support their comments with actions. It's more important to start taking action than wait for the complete plan.

"Implementation Never Goes According to Plan"

This is an expression I have been using for many years to explain that organizations must have the agility and ability to redirect actions and leverage situations.

In *Beyond Strategy–The Leader's Role in Successful Implementation,* I quoted Scotland's favorite poet Robert Burns: "The best laid schemes o'mice an' men/ Gang aft a-gley." Translated from Scottish, it means the *best laid plans of mice and men never go according to plan.* Similarly, after you have crafted the strategy, you need to recognize that whatever was planned will not be what happens in the execution.

There are few absolutes in business but this is one. Considerable forces affecting the strategy also affect the execution, and therefore it *will* change. That's why leaders have to remain agile and open-minded as they constantly review the execution.

> *Powerful Execution Tip*: Don't fall in love with the execution plan. It will change to identify if the *strategy* or the *execution* is wrong—or both.

Here are a few highly visible examples of when the execution didn't go according to plan.

Example #1: Heathrow Airport learned an embarrassing and costly lesson when it opened its fifth terminal in March 2008. The airport had promised a sparkling new efficient terminal that would provide a "much-improved" experience for passengers. It was designed to handle 45 million passengers a year and 12,000 bags an hour. Before its opening, then British Airways CEO Willie Walsh went on global television declaring, "Three years of planning . . . we're waiting for the day . . . We have worked through every scenario . . . We believe we are ready."

The reality? On the second day of the terminal's opening, 70 flights were cancelled and 30,000 bags were mislaid. The terminal became known as a hotel for the stranded. The cost of this failure was £62 million. In the words of Walsh, "It was *not* our finest hour." A well-thought-out strategy was poorly executed.

Example #2: In 2002, the German retail chain Metro became the first foreign distributor to enter Vietnam. The retailer promised a new kind of shopping experience for the country. Yet when the doors opened, hardly any customers came to buy. Metro had spent considerable time and money preparing to enter the market, but despite this, their execution faltered initially due to missteps.

Specifically, Metro stationed uniformed security guards at the entrance for security—not an unusual practice in retail stores in some countries. But in Vietnam, the practice evoked memories of the country's former totalitarian rule, and it stopped potential customers from entering. Those who did enter experienced an unfamiliar shopping experience. For example, tomatoes were already packaged and not laid out for them to select as they were used to. Some customers were suspicious of this new layout and tore open the packets, thinking the store was hiding rotten tomatoes beneath fresh-looking ones. Metro had to give up the plastic packaging and stack the tomatoes the way they usually were at a farm stall. Also, when the passengers saw signs saying "fresh chicken," they expected fresh chickens still alive, not packaged!

Example #3: McDonald's initiated a growth strategy for China in 1992. At the time, it was playing catch-up to Kentucky Fried Chicken that had already entered China. As part of the strategy to maximize customer revenue, McDonald's introduced the "drive-through" concept, and individual locations were refurnished to accommodate drive-through orders.

One day, a manager was outside watching to see how the new revenue-producing idea was performing. A customer drove up to the machine, placed his order, and drove forward to collect his meal and pay for it. The astonished manager then watched as the customer parked his car in the car park, picked up his brown bag, walked into the restaurant and sat down to eat his meal.

McDonald's had not only introduced the first fast food drive-through but the very first drive-through in all of China. The strategy of maximizing revenue by having customers purchase their meal and eat it outside did not go according to plan.

Example #4: The French railway had a plan to improve its trains, the regional network and accessibility for disabled to attract more passengers. When the plan was implemented in 2014, the 2,000 new trains that cost $20 billion were too wide for the platforms.

What happened? They had measured the distance between the platforms at the stations built about 30 years ago. But in the south of France and other areas, more than a 1,000 stations that had been built 50 years before when the platform distances were less. The blunder cost over $70 million to correct as 1,300 platforms had to be rebuilt. And it got worse. The new trains were several millimeters too tall to go through the tunnels in Italy, forcing passengers to change to shorter trains at the border.

Leaders need to be constantly engaged throughout the implementation journey, ensuring the actions are achieving the desired outcomes. The next chapter introduces areas in which leaders regularly struggle with, how to translate the strategy into every day actions and resolve the challenge by leveraging and adopting the Three Broad Themes of Execution and the Implementation Compass™. It also discusses the speed of your execution and how to assess your execution capabilities.

—— *Chapter Five* ——

Strategy@50,000 Feet
to Ground Level

 Video Question: 95% of people in an organization can't tell you what?

S trategy is crafted at 50,000 feet and is executed at the ground level."
This an expression I use to explain the elevated view required by
leaders. The challenge is to ensure people on the ground understand
the strategy and take the right actions. This requires substantially more focus
from leaders than it typically receives.

Introducing the Three Broad Themes of Execution

Since 2000, Bridges' research and client work has allowed us to observe,
analyze and participate in Excellence in Execution. When we reviewed the
practices of organizations and spoke to leaders, we discovered they were
struggling to make this 50,000-foot translation. Examining and working
with successful organizations, we identified three common broad themes

present throughout the process of translating the strategy into action. These themes provided the structure and enabled leaders to communicate the strategy. They also inspired the right actions and created traction throughout the implementation journey.

The Three Broad Themes of Execution are:

1. **Create Awareness**
2. **Build Excellence**
3. **Follow Through**

In many situations, translating the strategy to the people at ground level is unstructured. It involves leaders conducting different initiatives in silos, different training and varied communication and measurement. The lack of structured activities can cause the execution to be random and chaotic. See Figure 5.1 that shows the organization taking random actions in different directions.

Figure 5.1

Strategy@50,000ft

Unstructured

Execution

Ground Level

The Three Broad Themes of Execution provide a structured, high-level understanding of why the organization was changing. What needed to be done is shown in Figure 5.2.

Figure 5.2

Strategy@50,000ft

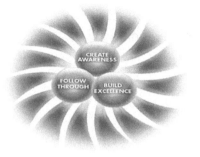

Structured

Execution

Ground Level

The themes also assist leaders to bring the strategy from 50,000 feet high (as seen by senior leaders) down to ground level (where it's executed by those on the front line). They serve as a bridge between the strategy and its execution. More than that, they assist in decoding the execution challenge, making it easier to understand the journey ahead.

Create Awareness

Leaders know that creating an awareness of the new strategy among employees is important, but they tend to be weak at doing it because many equate building awareness with giving a speech, attending meetings, or sending emails. Ironically, they spend months and sometimes years crafting the strategy, and then they take only a short time to explain to their **People** the **Biz Case**, the reason the organization must transform. They expect them to act on the execution with the same commitment, drive and passion they have. This "disconnect" harms the execution before it even starts.

From our latest research, we discovered that only 5% of people can articulate their own organization's strategy. *This is the answer to this chapter's video question.*

Creating awareness largely overcomes this.

Build Excellence

Once people have an awareness of *why* the organization is transforming, *why* they should participate in the execution, *what* their new role is and *what* actions they should take, it's imperative to Build Excellence. Far too often after a strategy launch, people go "back to business as usual" within a few months. There simply hasn't been enough engagement.

To Build Excellence and ensure traction, it's critical to **Communicate** what's working, including the lessons learned. Sharing best practices and conveying next steps are also requirements. To ensure the new strategy is being tracked properly, the **Measures** must be reviewed and changed when required. Because an organization's **Culture** drives the way the execution happens, all aspects of its culture need to be examined. Two organizations can have the same strategy but because each has a unique culture, how they each achieve Excellence in Execution is different. Leaders must make the execution their own.

Building engagement also requires empowering people to change/innovate their work **Processes**. By definition, when you launch a new strategy, you're asking people to work *differently*. Therefore, the people on the ground need to be empowered to remove obsolete processes and initiate improvements. To empower people requires putting in place the right support structure—including how to handle the situation when it fails.

Follow Through

Once engagement is built, how do you maintain and sustain the momentum? After all, Excellence in Execution doesn't happen in a few weeks or months; it takes years. Leaders keep the fire of enthusiasm alive by funneling the flames with regular **Reinforcement** and **Review**.

It's essential to reinforce the right actions *when they are taken*. People who are early adopters of the execution need encouragement to take risks. When they don't receive support, they stop doing the right things and momentum is lost.

Also, a regular **Review** of the execution is necessary to provide feedback, make corrections, hold people accountable and keep all activity relevant. Excellence in Execution requires constant modifications to remain on target.

In some organizations, reviews are carried out only once or twice a year. By that time, minor problems have likely ballooned into large ones—some large enough to derail the whole execution and miss the target. Therefore, conduct reviews regularly.

The Three Broad Themes of Execution assist in building your HOW and making sure you achieve Excellence in Execution. Leaders also have to consider the speed the organization should move through the three broad themes—the Strategy Cadence.

Strategy Cadence

Moving from Strategy@50,000 feet to ground level through the Three Broad Themes of Execution happens at a different pace for different organizations and different industries. I call this pace the Strategy Cadence, adopted from a term used in the sport of cycling to measure the rate a cyclist is pedaling.

The strategy itself and the urgency surrounding it dictate the pace Excellence in Execution moves. This includes assessment of your competition, scan of the market, customer reviews, financial analysis and other key factors that affect your strategy.

**Your organization's Strategy Cadence refers
to the rate at which the execution is happening.**

During the crafting of the strategy, leaders decide the Strategy Cadence, which has three execution gears:

1. Slow—more than five years
2. Medium—less than five years and more than three years
3. Fast—less than three years

Powerful Execution Tip: Strategy Cadence is driven by your business circumstances and urgency that are identified during the crafting of the strategy.

> "The speed and quality of Strategy Execution is the
> most important differentiator between competitors."
> —R. Michael Donovan & Co., Inc.

"Slow" Strategy Cadence—Snail
If you intentionally select a "Slow" Strategy Cadence, it may be because executing the new strategy is *not* urgent. Businesses in certain industries such as mining or agriculture or aircraft manufacturers might have up to 10 to 15 years to execute their strategies. This allows leaders the opportunity to discuss and engage various people in the strategy. The sense of urgency is low.

"Medium" Strategy Cadence—Rabbit
Most organizations have a "Medium" Strategy Cadence. That means every three to five years, they keep revisiting and crafting a new strategy. Financial institutions fall into this category.

During the Medium Strategy Cadence, leaders have only a few years to execute the new strategy. That pace requires more of an autocrat-style leadership compared to a slow Strategy Cadence. With a Medium Strategy Cadence, leaders are forced to drive the new strategy forward before products and/or services become obsolete and revenue streams vanish.

A higher number of organizations fall into the Medium Strategy Cadence than ever before because the strategic landscape is changing faster. They have had to develop agility to adjust to the accelerated pace of change. The sense of urgency is fairly high.

"Fast" Strategy Cadence—Cheetah
For some organizations, a five-year strategic plan—or even a three-year one—is a thing of the past; they require a "Fast" Strategy Cadence especially if they're under pressure because of losing market share, revenue and/or customers. Immediate corrective action is required, which carries a high risk without the luxury of time to study circumstances and involve a variety of people. These leaders have a very high sense of urgency and a need for speed.

One organization in Muscat, Oman, for example, had made some bad moves in the market. As a result, it lost its number one position and was leaking both revenue and customers. A new CEO was brought in, and he adopted a Fast Strategy Cadence. The main principles for change were crafted and the strategy was tested during the implementation journey. The leaders felt an intense pressure to act. During the execution, the CEO personally reviewed its progress every two weeks and made any adjustments required. The board had requested the new CEO first stop the leakage and then win back the lost market share, which he did achieve. In this situation, speed was everything.

Competitive Strategy is Dead!

Among those with a Fast Strategy Cadence is a group that considers competitive strategy dead. Indeed, these organizations rely fully on Excellence in Execution as their competitive advantage. Their industry is moving so rapidly that leaders have to think on their feet, constantly "hustling" until they get it right. Interestingly, Amar Bhidé coined the term "Hustle as Strategy," claiming the most successful organizations "concentrate on operating details and doing things well. Hustle is their style and their strategy."[22]

Startups fall into this category as well as organizations recognizing a greater payoff in reacting fast than planning thoroughly. Consider organizations that develop apps, for example. In this fast-paced industry, the thinking is "it's better to design a prototype and test it than spend months doing research on it."

**"If you aren't embarrassed by the first version
of your product, you shipped too late."
—Reid Hoffman, co-founder/chairman LinkedIn,
partner Greyloc venture capital firm**

While crafting your new strategy, it's important to consider if your organization's execution needs to move as a snail, a rabbit or a cheetah, as illustrated in Figure 5.3.

---

22   https://hbr.org/1986/09/hustle-as-strategy

Figure 5.3

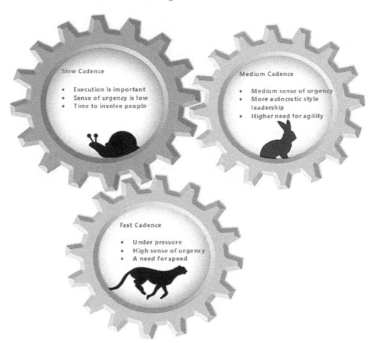

The Three Broad Themes of Execution are exactly that—broad themes that act as a stepping stone in starting to translate the strategy@50,000feet. Significantly more detail and structure is required as defined by the eight areas of Excellence in Execution and Part Two of the book.

The Eight Areas of Excellence in Execution

Execution frequently fails because leaders do *not* have a framework to guide them through their implementation journey. They are often left stumbling over the bridge between strategy and execution as they struggle to identify what to do and how to it.

Since 2002, Bridges has discovered from its research and client work that there are eight areas leaders must address to achieve Excellence in Execution. The research noted that organizations struggling to execute were addressing only a couple of the key areas. For example, they were sending employees for new skills training required or adopting a new scorecard or innovating. *But this was not enough.*

Excellence in Execution organizations perform across all eight areas. (Earlier in this chapter, the eight areas were subtly introduced under The Three Broad Themes of Execution and marked by bold type.) They address:

1. Engaging the **People**—The people, not the leaders, execute the strategy.
2. Sharing the **Biz Case**—A need to create a sense of urgency around why the organization must transform.
3. Constantly **Communicating**—Frequently explain what is happening, its impact and next steps.
4. Putting in place the right **Measures**—Track the progress through the implementation journey.
5. Aligning execution and **Culture**—An organization's culture drives the way execution happens and you need to make it your own.
6. Change and innovate **Processes**—Empowering people to improve the way they are working to support the new strategy.
7. **Reinforcing**—Encouraging the right actions across the organization.
8. **Reviewing**—Frequently monitoring the execution.

For a video introduction visit:
www.implementation-hub.com/implementation_framework

These eight areas of Excellence in Execution make up the Implementation Compass™, which is a framework for identifying the right actions to execute strategy and Bridges proprietary framework. There are other frameworks to consider such as Palladium Execution Premium Process™ (XPP)[23] developed by Drs. Robert S. Kaplan and David P. Norton and their Palladium associates. The model assists leader to clarify strategy, drive performance and optimize data.

For a video introduction visit:
www.youtube.com/watch?v=DpnCuoCY2Vs

---

23 http://www.thepalladiumgroup.com/knowledge/Palladium-Execution-Premium-Process-XPP

The Implementation Compass™

The Implementation Compass (Compass) was first published in 2004 in my book *Bricks to Bridges—Make Your Strategy Come Alive* as a metaphor for leaders to understand the eight areas of implementation. After being adopted by hundreds of organization from different industries around the world, its value remains constant.

The strategy created is your organization's map that shows *where you are* and *where you want to go*. The Compass shows you which actions to take to move toward your strategy in the right direction throughout the implementation journey. As a leader, you act as a guide showing people the best path to take.

> *Powerful Execution Tip*: Be conscious of all eight areas of Excellence in Execution that make up the Compass at all times.

The Compass assists in identifying the right actions to take but you still require discipline throughout the organization to carry them out.

A Need for Discipline

To first craft a winning strategy and then take the right actions requires discipline. It's not, however, easy to *identify* the right actions, and it's even tougher to get everyone in the organization to *take* the right actions.

It's the discipline of taking the right
that achieves Excellence in Execution.

For you to live a healthy lifestyle, discipline has to become part of your DNA. Along the way, you'll have many distractions. It takes focus, commitment and passion to overcome them and succeed where many fail. This is true for strategy execution, too, which is discussed in more detail in Chapter Seven.

Powerful Execution Tip: The correlation between the different directions on the Compass is unique to each organization.

Where Do You Start?

Achieving Excellence in Execution involves addressing multiple actions from multiple directions plus a transformation in thinking and approach. The Compass's circular shape reinforces this. (You can identify your starting point by conducting your organization's Readiness2Execute, described in the following section.) As a leader, it's your responsibility to identify the right direction *and* the right actions for people to take. The Compass graphic reinforces the idea that the needle can point to any particular element at any time.

Executing strategy is circular, not a linear, process.

Your implementation journey can start with any one of the eight areas on the Compass. Here are three examples.

Example #1: An organization in China had spent two years crafting its strategy with the assistance of an external consultancy. When Bridges conducted its Readiness2Execute, we discovered that although all the senior leaders knew the strategy, they had not fully considered the impact of the execution on their own business areas. In addition, they were weak in setting up the right measures. For this organization, the entry point on the Compass for executing the strategy was Measure.

By creating a Strategy Scorecard, we helped the leaders identify the impact of the strategy on their business area. From there, we created a balance of measures and assisted in translating the organization's strategy into the business operations.

Example #2: The execution entry point for a manufacturing company in Malaysia was Reviews on the Compass. In the opinion of the CEO, its previous execution had failed. He didn't want to make the same mistakes again nor could he afford to. In addition, he identified the Strategy Cadence as Medium to Slow for the new strategy.

We brought everyone together into half-day performance reviews to discuss what went wrong last time, what lessons had been learned and what needed to be done differently. They had to understand why a new strategy was essential for the survival of the business.

The inputs from the Review drove the design of the execution plan. Initial engagement was high as people felt the leaders had listened and adopted their feedback on the previous failure.

Example #3: Working with an Indian conglomerate that has offices in more than 30 counties, Bridges was challenged to support its rollout of a sustainability strategy. From our earliest discussions, it quickly became clear that the word "sustainability" was ambiguous; not even the core team could define it. The starting point for the organization was the Biz Case, then Communication. We designed a teaser campaign to introduce sustainability, a tag line to describe its meaning and a communication plan to explain the concept and how to be involved.

Three Broad Themes and Compass Actions

When the three themes are combined, they provide leaders with a broad perspective to oversee the whole implementation journey as well as detailed actions to move forward. This is illustrated in Figure 5.4.

Figure 5.4

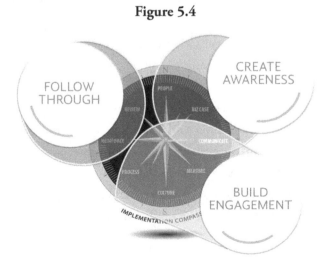

Create Awareness typically addresses the Compass elements of People, Biz Case and Communicate. Build Excellence requires continuing to Communicate and address Measure, Culture and Process. By focusing on Reinforce and Review, you Follow Through. However, there is no exact order in how to approach the journey. Leaders need to make the execution their own. As a leader, you can start by examining your own execution capabilities.

Readiness2Execute Assessment

How ready is your organization to implement the strategy?

Not all of the directions on the Implementation Compass are of equal importance to an organization at the same time, but all are important. An organization's leaders start by focusing on where best to spend their time and allocate their resources.

Powerful Execution Tip: Don't bet on your organization's future without assessing your execution capabilities and reassigning required resources.

Many organizations charge forward relying on past experience to make it work. They don't know, however, their current capabilities. This lack of knowledge contributes to the high failure rate. Just as you do due diligence before buying an organization or assess the market before launching a new product, you need to assess your execution capabilities before launching the new strategy.

By conducting a Readiness2Execute assessment, or engaging Bridges[24] to do so, you are able to customize your execution and build a detailed HOW (How Organizations Win). It evaluates the organization against the eight areas of Excellence in Execution as you examine (over approximately two weeks) the strategy plans and current business performance. During that time, you host focus groups and one-on-ones at all levels across the organization.

---

24   Contact bridges@bridgesconsultancy.com for more information.

Once completed, all results are transferred into a report and a radar diagram, which visually illustrates the organization's strengths and weaknesses. By taking time to understand the organization's strengths and weaknesses, you are building a HOW that sets up your organization for success. In effect, you know what to do and what not to do.

The radar illustration in Figure 5.5 is an example of an organization's score from the assessment.

Figure 5.5

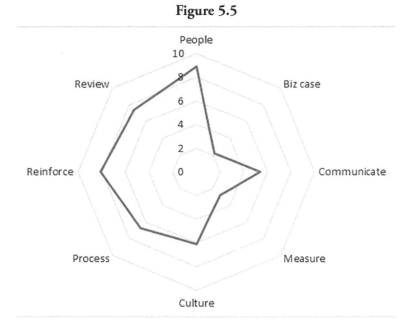

From this example, you see the two major areas of concern are:

- Biz Case—people do not understand why the organization needs to change
- Measure—the organization needs to review the measures and how they are being used

The two major strengths are:

- People—highly driven and skilled
- Reinforce—people feel appreciated for their efforts

Once the assessment has been completed, the leadership team then leverages the information to develop the HOW. Often leaders assume they are doing better than they are, so the assessment often works as a reality check. From this assessment, the leadership team can determine the right actions to rectify the weaknesses and support the strengths as they start to build the execution plan.

Sample the assessment for your organization at, www.bridgesconsultancy.com/readiness2execute-assessment-tool

Chapter Six introduces the Strategy Execution Skills Gap, Execution Juxtaposition, Strategy Execution Office, Middle Managers Influence and the Strategic Priorities Exercise.

Chapter Six

Bridging the Skills Gap

Video: How do middle managers persuade people to take the right actions?

*W*hat's required to achieve Excellence in Execution has not been taught in the classroom. New thinking, tools and techniques need to be adopted.

Strategy Execution Skills Gap

There's a precarious gap in leader's capabilities to understand how to decode execution. While earning a business degree, they might have attended a module on operations management or change management, but this is different from strategy execution. On the faculty of business schools, they'd find a *strategy* professor but rarely an *execution* professor. As a result, the current generation of leaders has been taught how to *create* a plan but not how to *execute* it. This has generated a Strategy Execution Skills Gap that causes leaders to struggle through the implementation journey.

Powerful Execution Tip: A key difference in today's market between you and your competition is the ability to execute. Your organization will be left behind if your competition implements strategy better than you do, so make sure everyone has the skills to execute.

It's essential for organizations to bridge the Strategy Execution Skills Gap by providing leaders with the required knowledge and skills. For example, Oracle has made 100 acquisitions during a recent five-year period. To support the organization's leaders to execute the strategy and bridge the gap, it conducted a program called Leading to Win in Asia Pacific, which Bridges was involved with. It focused on collaboration and learning the skills of execution.

Bridges offers varies courses to support filling the execution gap:

1. Strategy Implementation for Leaders—Addresses why change management does not work for implementation and shares the framework the Implementation Compass™ in an entertaining, engaging one-day seminar.

2. Middle Managers Role in Strategy Implementation—One-day workshop on how middle managers can influence change. It discusses the essential role they play, assesses their implementation skills and debriefs a case study.

3. Build Your Strategy Execution Plan—An in-house interactive two-day workshop for leadership teams to plan the execution before launching a new strategy.

4. Masterclass: How to Achieve Excellence in Execution—A highly informative and interactive three-day workshop to understand how to execute strategy and to leverage the mindset, toolset and skillset from successful organizations (based on this book). Visit www.bridgesconsultancy.com/category/bridges-courses/ for more information.

Sandeep Sander, CEO of SanderMan and a good friend, claims the missing execution competencies in the future will be covered through lifelong learning and that will lead to employability, a term explained in a YouTube video titled Employability.[25]

Lifelong learning is becoming a key element for successful execution because no education endures forever. At all levels and in all functions, people need to embark on a lifelong learning journey. Sometimes it takes the form of updates and upgrades within an area of expertise. More often, learning in additional subject areas is required to continue delivering excellence within any function.

Two key questions should form the basis for a lifelong learning plan, according to Sandeep, for each individual: 1) What am I aiming at? and 2) Where am I? Keeping up with learning demands feels like shooting toward a moving target—and the target itself is constantly transforming. Once this is defined (for now), then it is essential to get clarity on each person's present competence level in the relevant disciplines.

To support organizations to provide the execution competencies use:

 SanderMan's Cloud Solution (www.sanderman.com)

SanderMan's cloud solution provides an overview for the individual *and* overall application. For each person, the starting point includes noting the "ideal competencies" required, which depend on industry, level and function. Each person is then empowered to make a self-assessment of the actual level. The gaps are identified in this way. The software then presents a short list of learning options tailored to the organization and the person. It also enables leaders and the HR staff to receive the overview and features built-in workflows.

Even when leaders possess the skills required, they still face a conflict on what to focus on within their organization.

The Execution Juxtaposition

Leaders commonly face a juxtaposition in execution. Juxtaposition is a literary term referring to two or more ideas and/or actions placed side by side. For

25   https://www.youtube.com/watch?v=2xf4nX5O378 and https://en.wikipedia.org/wiki/Employability

example, a poster warning about children obesity is incongruently placed next to an advertisement for fast food.

When leaders execute a *long-term* strategy but are measured and rewarded for *short-term* performance, this creates a tense juxtaposition that many organizations fail to address. They become fixated on what's wrong today and lose sight of what's right for tomorrow.

**If you only focus on running the business,
you will run it into the ground.**

It takes discipline to defend your position every quarter while balancing the long view with quarterly performance. It's even tougher when resources are allocated and goals are set for short-term performance. This is one of the main reasons an execution loses traction and frequently fails.

Powerful Execution Tip: The pressure of delivering quarterly results is the downfall of many a strategy execution.

Steve Ballmer when he was CEO of Microsoft tripled the sales of the organization but under his stewardship Microsoft missed many of the future technology trends. For example, Microsoft should have transferred their dominance of computer Operating Systems to mobile but have not and they were beaten in search by Google.

Leaders spend their time and energy fighting against the execution juxtaposition. For example, they might present and defend quarterly performance and not discuss the execution of the strategy objectives. To manage the juxtaposition, some organizations create a dedicated strategy execution office.

Strategy Execution Office
In some organizations an office dedicated to the execution assists in ensuring the organization has a balance in its approach and both a short-

term and long-term perspective. It also ensures the organization adopts the discipline and best practices required to succeed while coordinating plans and communication.

Setting up a Strategy Execution Office is not the right approach for every organization. Some leaders argue they need an additional focus on structure and discipline that a dedicated Strategy Execution Office can provide. The opposing argument is that execution is the responsibility of everyone, not only one office. Just as noted for strategy planning and quality improvement, everyone must own the execution.

General Electric (GE) famously dissolved its strategic planning (originally called long-range planning) under Jack Welch's stewardship because its leaders wanted *everyone* to be responsible for strategic planning. Welch threw out GE's elaborative five-year planning documents and replaced them with a simple statement of business challenges and proposed action plans.

The same debate surfaced again around quality improvement. Should organizations set up a central quality office or is everyone responsible for quality? The question for Excellence in Execution is, should there be a specific office to drive and champion it? After all, isn't execution the responsibility of everyone? With a Strategy Execution Office in place, there's a deep concern that people will say, "It's not my responsibility" and expect those in the office to do everything.

The answer to this question lies in your organization's approach to making the execution your own. To assist in the discussion, consider the following list of responsibilities for the Strategy Execution Office.

 Strategy Execution Office Responsibilities

The responsibilities include:

- ✓ Connect the corporate strategy to the lines of business (e.g., communicate and explain what needs to be achieved).
- ✓ Report directly to the CEO.

✓ Develop and champion the strategy management process and system.

✓ Close any gaps between crafting strategy and execution.

✓ Manage organizational alignment with the strategy.

✓ Assist in execution planning (e.g., provide standard templates).

✓ Keep execution on the leaders' radar e.g., influence meeting agendas.

✓ Provide guidance and support throughout the implementation journey.

✓ Ensure regular execution reviews are conducted.

✓ Champion, standardize and manage strategic measures.

✓ Prepare regular assessment meetings.

✓ Ensure execution governance is in place.

✓ Share best practices and lessons learned across all lines of business.

✓ Review the strategic landscape outside the organization.

If you do opt to create a Strategy Execution Office, then aim to make it obsolete within a few years (depending on your Strategy Cadence). By then, the knowledge, skills and discipline should be transferred to those in various lines of business.

A critical role in decoding execution that's sometimes overlooked is the role played by middle managers.

Middle Managers Influence

With leaders driving and championing their people, the role of middle managers is often not given adequate attention. That can jeopardize the execution's success.

Powerful Execution Tip: If middle managers are not supported as the lynchpins of execution, then it will fail.

In running the business, people will turn to their immediate boss for guidance in making everyday decisions. They will also require coaching and guidance when wrong decisions are made. Middle managers have to know the organization's priorities so they can guide people in the right direction and take the right actions. Yet various research studies reveal that less than half of the middle managers are able to name the organization's top five priorities.

Despite all the communication from senior leaders, most middle managers don't know their own organization's top priorities. This can derail the execution effort.

 ### The Role of a Middle Manager

✓ Middle managers advance Excellence in Execution in these ways:
✓ Explain the new strategy to their people in detail.
✓ Align the strategic priorities.
✓ Discuss how the strategy affects their people.
✓ Further explain what is expected of them.
✓ Link the strategy to the day-to-day business.
✓ Assist people in adopting the right actions.
✓ Listen to their employees' grievances.
✓ Model the right actions.
✓ Identify and provide required training and coaching.
✓ Become project leaders.
✓ Engage people in decisions rather than dictate to them.
✓ Review their employees' performances regularly.
✓ Reinforce the right actions.
✓ Provide feedback to leaders on the progress throughout the implementation journey.

"Execution should be driven from the middle."
—Donald Sull, Rebecca Homkes, Charles Sull

Can Middle Managers Create Change?

A common question among middle managers is, "Can I create change at my level?" The answer is "yes"; it happens by creating success within their area of influence to the point that other leaders ask, "How did you do it?"

Success sells, theory promises.

This success then makes it easier to convince others to change, which involves persuading the manager's own people to do things differently. Jennifer Overbeck, a social psychologist and associate professor of management at Melbourne Business School, published an excellent article titled "You Don't Have to Be the Boss to Change How Your Company Works."[26] In it, Overbeck states that to bring your people on board, start by changing their attitudes that will, in turn, drive their actions. She refers to the work of psychologists Muzafer Sherif and Carl Hovland and their "latitude of acceptance" principle. This claims people will entertain new ideas but only when they fall within a narrow range of one's own attitude.

**Persuading people to participate in the change
requires small steps to bring them along.** *This is
the answer to this chapter's video question.*

Thus, when wanting to persuade others to participate, Overbeck lists these actions to avoid:

- Trying to achieve "conversion" and not just progress. ("Don't expect to achieve all your goals in a single shot.")
- Talking to people who mostly agree with you.
- Trying to drive change without others' help.
- Relying primarily on email blasts.
- Motivating change by appealing to lofty principles.

Even if it takes extra time and patience, doing it right is worth the effort.

---

26 https://hbr.org/2015/02/you-dont-have-to-be-the-boss-to-change-how-your-company-works

Bridging the Communication Chasm

Middle managers bridge the communication chasm not only by being more effective in their communication but by understanding the strategic priorities of the execution. That's how they can ensure the right actions are being taken while providing corrective feedback throughout the journey.

As evidence, a McKinsey & Company study[27] found that supervisors and managers who oversee the work of frontline employees spend more than half their time in administrative tasks, meetings, filing reports and travel—all things that compete with coaching and mentoring their people. In the worst cases, these tasks consume 90% of a manager's time. Supervisor time spent with frontline workers varies by industry. In the airline industry, for example, many travelers will not be surprised that the record of the airline industry is the worst. There, supervisors spend at most only 10% to 15% of the time with frontline employees.

Only 15% of people in an organization can identify their organization's most important goals and priorities, according to Franklin Covey's research.[28]

Powerful Execution Tip: Translating strategy into action requires middle managers to clarify individual responsibilities and expected outcomes to the people who report to them.

Once traction is gained, middle managers coach their people along the journey by sharing best practices, learning from mistakes, removing roadblocks and providing feedback. The coaching provides positive feedback and creates the conditions that encourage participation in the execution.

The larger the organization, the more dependent it becomes on middle managers and their abilities to lead. Middle managers are sometimes called the "thermal layer" because they absorb information from above and below. They hear the challenges people face integrating the execution process into their everyday

---

27 http://www.mckinsey.com/insights/organization/unlocking_the_potential_of_frontline_managers
28 http://www.connectionsonline.net/news/strategy-execution.aspx

work. They also provide feedback up the chain of management to explain what's happening, and they convey critical information from management to their people. Paying attention to the role of middle managers does not *guarantee* Excellence in Execution. Ignoring their role, however, makes the challenge extremely harder.

Once people start to support a certain direction, you can assist them to understand the priorities. It is therefore important to ensure you are working on the right priorities, which can be achieved by conducting a priorities exercise.

Strategic Priorities Exercise (SPE)

This exercise helps leaders identify discrepancies people have understanding the organization's strategic priorities. It ensures everyone knows what is important.

 Strategic Priorities Exercise

Follow these steps to prioritize each activity:

1. Identify the top five priorities of the strategy execution for yourself.
2. Ask the CEO, "What are your top five priorities to execute the strategy?"
3. Ask the CEO's direct reports, "What are the organization's top five priorities to execute the strategy?"
4. Ask middle managers what they see as the top five priorities to execute the strategy.
5. Host a meeting to review, identify and resolve any discrepancies to ensure everyone's priorities are aligned.

In their book *The 4 Disciplines of Execution*[29] Chris McChesney, Sean Covey, and Jim Huling made these points:

- Only one in seven people can name the organization's most important goal.

---

29 Chris McChesney, Sean Covey, Jim Huling. *The 4 Disciplines of Execution: Achieving Your Wildly Important Goals*. Free Press, 2012.

- Only 51% of those who knew about the goals were passionate about achieving them.
- 87% of people had no clear idea what action they should take.

Chapter Seven delves deeper into the discipline of taking the right actions.

Chapter Seven

Eight Building Blocks to Taking the Right Actions

 Video question: How can you increase the probability of people taking the right actions by fivefold?

*I*f strategy is about making the right choices, then execution is about taking the right actions. Strategy focuses on *thinking*; execution centers on *doing,* and many people struggle with identifying the right actions. Achieving Excellence in Execution requires cultivating a bias toward action across the organization. As David M. Cote, CEO of Honeywell, said, "The trick is in the doing."

The discipline of taking the right actions is captured in the story of how Peter Rosengard entered the *Guinness Book of Records* for selling the world's largest life insurance policy. In a cold call made from a London phone box in 1991, he sold a 100-million-dollar policy to insure music mogul David Geffen. Here's how it happened.

In 1990, Peter read in the British newspapers that MCA Universal had taken over Geffen Records in Los Angeles, California. Instead of reading the headline and moving on, Peter took action. He knew the name David Geffen was synonymous with identifying musical talent and making money-spinning deals. So he deduced that MCA Universal's decision-makers were investing more in one person than they would in a company. Peter had the audacity to go to a public phone box (remember, it was 1990) and call MCA Universal directly. He didn't ask for the finance or human resources heads; instead, he went straight to the office of Sid Sheinberg, the president. Not surprisingly, the president's gatekeeper blocked him from speaking to Mr. Sheinberg.

Many people would have given up at this point, but top sales people keep coming back—on average five times. Peter proved himself to definitely be a top salesperson.

Next, from the phone box in London, England, he made almost two dozen cold calls around the offices MCA Universal. He eventually learned Mr. Sheinberg was attending a film festival in Florence, Italy.

Many people would have decided to wait until Mr. Sheinberg returned to the U.S., but no one gets into the *Guinness Book of Records* by doing what everyone else does.

Peter realized that a man of Mr. Sheinberg's stature could only be staying at one of a select few hotels in Florence. So he called the elite hotels and asked to speak to the concierge. Because Peter has a regular breakfast table at Claridges in London, he was able to leverage his knowledge about the Golden Keys, a global association for concierge, in his conversations. This helped him befriend the concierge who revealed Mr. Sheinberg was a guest in his hotel.

Next, Peter called that hotel at seven in the evening Florence time. Why that time? He predicted Mr. Sheinberg would be back in his room after a day of meetings. He'd be changing his clothes to go out for dinner and, most important, he'd be without his entourage. He guessed right. Sid Sheinberg picked up the phone in his room.

Peter congratulated Sid (he used Mr. Sheinberg's first name) on the Geffen deal. Then he said he had an idea that would be tremendously valuable to MCA and made a promise. He'd ask Sid only one question, and if he was wrong about Sid's answer, he'd hang up. Peter's question was, "If David Geffen walked under a truck tonight on the Santa Monica Boulevard and was killed, am I right in assuming MCA would have just lost hundreds of millions dollars?" He then remained silent, which was not easy to do.

Sid finally spoke. He said that was true, and then he asked what Peter suggested be done. The insurance salesman recommended not a one-million-dollar life insurance policy but a *hundred-million-dollar* policy. After all, David Geffen was worth millions to MCA.

All the while, Peter tried to control his voice as if it were natural for him to handle such a huge policy. Sid asked a few clarifying questions and then told Peter to call MCA's chief financial officer. Peter quickly asked for his approval to tell the CFO they had spoken.

By serendipity, the CFO was in the U.K. at the time. The next morning, Peter was hosting the CFO for breakfast at his regular table at Claridges Hotel.

MCA's executive team was already considering buying a policy, so achieving this sale could be simply explained by excellent timing. But more than that, it was Peter's steadfast *bias for action* that took him through each stage of selling the biggest insurance policy in the world—a record that stands today.

As the story explains, Peter had to make key choices and take the right actions at several precarious crossroads along the way. The same is required from leaders along the implementation journey and doing so takes discipline. It's too simple to do the opposite of action.

If you had to choose, would you say it's better to take the wrong actions or no action at all? Taking the *wrong* actions is better than inertia because the momentum of taking action already exists in the culture.

The Eight Building Blocks

To ensure the right actions are being taken and against inertia, execute the eight building blocks for developing the discipline in an organization illustrated in Figure 7.1.

Figure 7.1

1. The Discipline

Everyday people are busy, but are the actions they take the *right* actions that are executing the strategy? With so much to do each day, it becomes harder and harder to make decisions and direct the actions to keep the long-term strategy view in place.

Also, just because people know what to do does not mean they are doing it. *Knowing* what to do and actually *doing* it are two very different things. CEB research[30] indicates that more than half of employees are less focused on the right activities and do not feel aligned with corporate priorities.

---

30   https://www.cebglobal.com/exbd/workforce-surveys-analytics/business-priorities/index.page

---

**"The truth of the matter is that you always know
the right thing to do. The hard part is doing it."
—General H. Norman Schwarzkopf, U.S. Army**

To ensure the right actions are being taken to execute, an organization needs to instill the discipline—often lacking. This involves ensuring people know what the right actions are and are inspired to act.

Leaders who drive and champion execution need to instill the required discipline by adopting the eight building blocks. As Jim Rohn is quoted as saying, "You can either choose the pain of discipline or the pain of regret."[31]

Powerful Execution Tip: The right actions have a disproportional impact on the execution. With Excellence in Execution in place, 20% of the right effort can produce 80% of the results, so make sure your people are taking the right actions.

Adopting the discipline takes focus and effort. The reward is the payoff in achieving success where so many others fail, and that payoff can be in the billions of dollars of profits.

2. Double Paradox of Choice

Choice is a double paradox because people are more likely to take the right actions if they have choices. Yet when they have too many choices, they do nothing!

It's important to offer people choices. They're more committed to outcomes they set themselves by a ratio of almost five to one, as noted by Carolyn Aiken and Scott Keller from McKinsey & Company in their paper "The irrational side of change management."[32] *This is the answer to this chapter's video question.*

The authors cite a famous behavioral experiment in which half the participants are randomly assigned a lottery ticket number while the others are asked to

---

31 http://thinkexist.com/quotation/we-must-all-suffer-from-one-of-two-pains-the-pain/347821.html
32 http://www.mckinsey.com/insights/organization/the_irrational_side_of_change_management

write down any number they would like on a blank ticket. Just before drawing the winning number, the researchers offer to buy back the tickets from their holders. The result: no matter what geography or demographic environment the experiment has taken place in, researchers have found they have to pay at least *five times more* to those who came up with their own number. Why? Because we are more dedicated to outcomes we set ourselves.

In organizations that have achieved Excellence in Execution, leaders plan to allow their people to choose how they participate in the execution to gain greater commitment. That means offering people two or three choices. For example, Infocomm in Singapore terminated its contract with a single IT vendor this year in favor of allowing each business unit to choose from three different vendors rather than being forced to use one vendor. (See also the Decoy Effect in this chapter as an example of giving people a choice.)

People commit more easily to taking the right actions when they can choose themselves what they need to do.

If you offer too many choices, then people do less, not more, and sometimes they do nothing. Research has also demonstrated that an excess of choices often leads to people being less, not more, satisfied once they actually decide. This is because of a nagging feeling they could have done better.

This principle applies in the same way for taking action. When you have too many actions to do, it becomes hard to focus on any one. The outcome can be nothing gets done. So aim to give few (not many) choices; three is ideal.

Too many choices in execution can lead to the same levels of lower employee engagement and satisfaction as not having any choice.

How many strategy objectives should you focus on each year?

The double paradox principle also applies for leaders selecting strategic objectives to work on every year. A strategy typically has many objectives over a few years—all deemed important. But they don't aim to execute everything immediately. When you have a few years to execute your strategy, the advice is to balance and limit what's expected every 12 months. Select the urgent and the immediate for each 12-month period.

This then begs the question, "How many strategic objectives should a leadership team focus on every 12 months?" The magic number is between three and five.

By focusing on between three and five, people don't feel overwhelmed with too much to do. It sends a clear and compelling message about what needs to be done most urgently. It also sets the tone for a high-performing culture, allows allocation of resources and develops the discipline to prioritize.

"There must be a certain balance to the number and type of goals and objectives: too many goals and objectives are paralyzing; too few, confusing."
—Professor Kathleen Eisenhardt, Stanford University

An experiment by Sheena S. Iyengar (Columbia University) and Mark R. Lepper (Stanford University) explained how less is more in their paper "When Choice is Demotivating: Can One Desire Too Much of a Good Thing?"[33]

They wrote about the Jam Experiment that involved an upscale grocery store displaying, on one occasion, 24 jams for customers to view and purchase and, on the other occasion, only six different jams. From the customers who visited the 24-jam selection, only 3% purchased. From the six jam selection, 30% of the customers purchased. That's 10 times more.

The experiment also tested for choices of chocolate. Once again, the group being offered only six choices had a higher level of satisfaction and sales than those offered more choices.

National Geographic reported on a similar experiment for its program Brain Games. They selected two ice cream parlors. One only offered three flavors and the other many different flavors. Researchers concluded that the brain prefers to choose from only three options.

---

33 https://faculty.washington.edu/jdb/345/345%20Articles/Iyengar%20%26%20Lepper%20(2000).pdf

In this program, Daylian Cain from Yale University explained why. The brain uses two systems to make choices. System one is automatic and unconscious; system two is deliberate and controlled (the one used in decision making). People might assume more choices will make them happier, but this isn't true. In fact, more choices make them unhappier. And having too much choice can be a hindrance.[34]

When applied to leaders executing strategy objectives, the conclusions from Iyengar and Lepper and the National Geographic indicate that leaders who focus on between three to five strategy objectives in 12 months get more done than those who focus on many more. When organizations try to execute more than 10 objectives, less gets done and in some cases, none of the objectives are completed. People working on them are so overwhelmed, they do a little on everything and nothing is finished.

In achieving Excellence in Execution, it is important to provide choices. People like having choices! So don't be the Henry Ford of execution offering only black as a choice. Also limit the number of choices and strategy objectives people have, to create a greater probability of the right actions moving into motion.

3. Right Actions in Motion

When you ask people to take an action that is small and manageable, there is a higher probability of them doing it than if the action is complicated and time consuming. Ask people to "boil the pot, not an ocean."

Dr. Robert Cialdini (Arizona State University) demonstrated the importance of setting parameters by showing how one small change delivered drastically different results. He reviewed the donation process of the American Cancer Society. His researchers asked for donations using two different phrases:

1. "Would you be willing to help by giving a donation?"
2. "Would you be willing to help by giving a donation? Every penny will help."

---

34 http://tvblogs.nationalgeographic.com/2013/06/03/three-ways-to-ease-decision-making/

Almost twice as many people who were asked the second question donated money than those asked the first question (50% versus 28%). By adding the minimum parameter of "even a penny," the request for action became more achievable.

**Encourage your people to participate in the execution
by stating what small action makes a good start.**

Powerful Execution Tip: Small actions by lots of people will result in a big change.

Bob Proctor's book *It's Not About The Money* notes the following from a Brigham Young University 1993 study[35] that identified what it takes to put action in motion:

- Those who made the statement, "That's a good idea," only had a 10% chance of making a change.
- Those who committed and said "I'll do it" had a 25% chance of making a change.
- Those who said *when* they would do it had a 40% chance of making a change.
- Those who set a specific plan of how to do it had a 50% chance of making a change.
- Those who committed to someone else that they would do it had a 60% chance of making a change.
- Those who set a specific time to share their progress with someone else had a 95% chance of making a change.

**The study emphasizes that, to have action in motion,
people need to know they are going to be asked by
their boss at a specific time on their progress.**

---

35 http://www.amazon.com/Its-About-Money-Your-Coach/dp/1596593768

Powerful Execution Tip: After agreeing the action your people should take to execute the strategy, set a date and time that you will review their progress within 90 days.

When you have thousands of people to influence, different tactics are required. Following are three more different choices you can choose from:

1. The Decoy Effect
2. Out for Lunch
3. Priming People

 The Decoy Effect

This is when rather than giving people two options, you add a third choice. This allows a comparison of A or B against C. Three choices can be better than two when it enables you to steer people toward doing what you really want them to do. Some people may consider this manipulation, but when you are betting the future of the organization and have to influence thousands of people, it's time to consider different tactics.

National Geographic's Brain Games researchers conducted an experiment in which they offered people entering a movie theatre two choices of popcorn: small for $3 and large for $7. Most people selected the small popcorn. But the movie theatre wanted to sell the larger popcorn because it made more profit. To achieve this, it introduced a third option, a medium popcorn at $6.50—the decoy. Why? Because suddenly the medium-priced popcorn made the large popcorn seem like a better value.

When you are faced with a tough decision between two options, introducing a third option adds information not previously considered. Typically, it leads people to make decisions more quickly.

You can use the decoy effect to accelerate your people into taking the right action. Like the popcorn example, you would create three execution experiences to choose from. They are:

- Intentionally imbalance what is being asked.
- Make the decoy action only marginally better than the action you want people to take.
- Make your decoy unreasonable.

 Out for Lunch

To set the right actions in motion, you can first do a small favor such as stay back to assist them when they are busy or take them out for lunch.

Dennis Regan, a researcher at Cornell University, conducted an experiment with two people selling raffle tickets to fellow workers. The first person was intentionally rude and the second was not. During a break, the rude person bought them drinks, and then they both tried to sell tickets again. The rude individual sold twice as many raffle tickets as the other person due to the Rule of Reciprocity.

This rule is prevalent in business. When a potential client is taken out for lunch, for example, this gift sets up an expectation to return the favor. Similarly, by doing your employees a small favor, they will feel more obligated to take the right actions for you.

 Priming People

This is providing a stimulus to improve the likelihood of people taking the right action. It subtly suggests an action and lays the groundwork for the eventual action.

In the 1980s, psychologists started finding that exposure to particular words could encourage recognition or evocation of related words more easily. For example, a person who sees the word "yellow" will be slightly faster to recognize the word "banana." This happens because the words "yellow" and "banana" are closely associated in memory.

John Bargh from Yale University conducted an experiment[36] when he was previously at New York University. He showed people a list of words that

---

36   http://www.yale.edu/acmelab/articles/bargh_chen_burrows_1996.pdf

appeared unrelated but were actually related. For example, on one sheet were words associated with old age. Professor Barge timed people walking into the room before the experiment and walking out after reading the words. Because of the words about old age, people walked out of the room at a slower pace and even acted older than before!

Consider the key actions you need people to take and how you can prime them by using the right images, stories and words.

4. Accountability

Adopting accountability is essential when striving to achieve Excellence in Execution. It requires holding someone responsible, with the emphasis on "one." Leaders hold each person accountable with constant follow through. Several experts agree that "holding people accountable for execution is one of the most powerful actions you can take."[37]

As MacDonald's CEO Steve Easterbrook replied when asked why revenues were declining and what had to change, "Our existing organization is inefficient and lacks clear accountability. We need to execute fewer things better.[38]

Creating accountability in your culture can make the difference between success and failure. My friend, Sam Silverstein, author of *Non-Negotiable*, put it this way when I am asked him about this topic: "There is a difference between accountability and responsibility. You are responsible for *things* and accountable to *people*. That report is not going to hold you accountable but your co-worker will. Accountability is keeping your commitments to people. Those commitments may be spoken like 'I will meet you at 11:00.' Some commitments are unspoken like 'I will value you as a person,' or, as the leader, 'I will make sure you are in a position to succeed.' When we take the time to truly understand what our commitments are and then work to keep those commitments, we become accountable."

Creating a culture of accountability in your organization requires knowing what is important to the organization and inculcating it.

---

37 Bougeois & Brodwin 1984, Alexander 1991, Floyd & Wooldridge (1994), Grundy 1998, Noble 1999, Beer & Eisenstat 2000, Flood et al. 2000.

38 http://www.businessinsider.sg/heres-where-mcdonalds-went-wrong-2015-5/#. VwbuneQgpPY

Six Steps for Creating a Culture of Accountability

1. **Know the organization's core values.**—The values act as your guiding principles of what is important and acceptable.
2. **Clarify expectations.**—People need to know how they are expected to perform and what they're expected to deliver based on the values *before* they can be held accountable. For example, does accountability mean attending meetings on time and/or submitting reports on time and/or checking that the right actions have been taken?
3. **Adopt measures.**—Putting in place the right measures allows you to track performance, show what is important and hold people accountable.
4. **Assign one person.**—You can't have more than one person responsible because that eradicates the accountability.
5. **Conduct reviews.**—People need to know they will be asked how they did against the planned actions on a regular basis.
6. **Link actions to consequences.**—People have to be recognized in a positive way when they take the right actions. There also needs to be negative consequences for inertia or the wrong actions, and the consequences have to be aligned with the values.

"The single most important change in actions that needs to occur during a time of cultural transition is the shift to greater accountability."
—Roger Connors and Tom Smith, *The Oz Principle*

Powerful Execution Tip: People who take on accountability make things happen and produce results.

Some people in organizations view accountability with negative connotations. They assume it only happens when something goes wrong—that is, leaders hold people accountable only when there are mistakes or problems.

If this belief prevails, then the organization will struggle to deliver results. Excellence in Execution organizations leverage accountability as a powerful tool. They use it not for pinpointing faults but as an opportunity to drive the right actions. They adopt the Six Steps for Creating a Culture of Accountability and leverage them to encourage commitment from their people to take the right actions.

To create a culture of accountability, ensure people know they will be held accountable, and recognized based on the organization's values. Then they will start to commit.

5. Commitment to Action

People commit to taking the right actions when they perceive they themselves will benefit and are directly responsible (and held accountable). This is partly why so many leaders in the initial launch highlight the expected benefits from the new strategy.

To ensure people are committed and know what to do, avoid a common mistake of creating a complicated action plan. To encourage people to commit to taking the right actions, the action plan should be easy to:

- Read
- Identify responsibility
- Adopt

A worthy action plan has only four columns with four question headings: What's the action? What is the outcome? When will it be achieved? Who is responsible? (See Figure 7.2 on the next page.)

To create an effective action plan, be sure to:

- Give each **action** its own line.
- Make sure the **outcome** is specific.
- Set the **completion date** within 90-days.
- Assign only one person to be **responsible**.

Figure 7.2

Action	Outcome	Completion Date	Responsible Person

The simpler the action plan and the easier it is to read, the more likely people will commit to action.

6. 90 Day Chunks

Plan to take action over a 90-day period. This is one of the most powerful principles for achieving Excellence in Execution. Why? There's something magic about setting actions to be completed in 90-day chunks within business. If a task is not completed within that timeframe, then:

- It might not have been important enough to demand your attention, or
- It was too complicated, or
- It requires more than 90-days and should have been broken down into smaller actions.

By consciously ensuring the actions can be completed within 90-day chunks, leaders make the actions manageable, and they start to gain traction. Theory promises and success sells. In this situation, the *strategy* is the theory and the *execution* is where success occurs by completing the action in 90-days.

Taking action in 90-day chunks makes the long-term strategy realistic to the people responsible for executing it and creates quick wins that people can see.

Powerful Execution Tip: Setting 90-day bite-size goals makes it easier to communicate the organization's most important objectives.

People identify their action by asking this question: "What can I do in the next 90-days to execute the strategy?"

Some people struggle with this question because they don't see how their work contributes to the strategy or because they don't believe they should do anything differently. It's important, therefore, for them to report to their immediate supervisor—the person they listen to most—and discuss what action to take toward executing the strategy. Their supervisors can assist them in identifying the right actions. During the 90-days, they constantly check in to see how they are progressing while offering support and guidance. The agreed-upon actions are captured by supervisors so they can hold people accountable. Also, not all the actions will be the right ones or create the expected outcomes. This is why supervisors need to constantly review what is happening.

The aim of insisting on (at least) one action every 90-days is to have as many people as possible participating in the execution.

7. Resources to Take the Right Actions

To demonstrate the importance of the new strategy, be sure to identify and allocate the resources required to support the right actions.

Excellence in Execution organizations focus first on freeing up the *required* resources, such as technology, people, time and financial assets. This can be hard to do. In some organizations, leaders set the budget, then plan the strategy but resources may not be available if they are not budgeted for. This is why it is best to craft the strategy and then set the budget. Kaplan and Norton state that 60% of organizations don't link budgets to strategy.[39]

---

39   https://hbr.org/2005/10/the-office-of-strategy-management

> **It's a leader's job to proactively manage essential capabilities such as budget and resources. They drive the organization's performance and ensure desired outcomes are delivered.**

Ankur Agrawal, Emma Gibbs and Jean-Hugues Monier commented in a 2016 *HBR* post, this way: "Companies tend to be timid capital reallocators. On average, they put 90% or more of their resources toward the same activities year after year, even though shifting resources as the business environment and company strategies change tends to deliver better, less volatile returns—particularly during down times."[40]

Execution often fails because of a lack or resource availability.

> **"Companies that are great at both strategy and execution marshal their resources strategically, doubling down on the few capabilities that matter most and pruning back everything else."**
> **—Paul Leinwand, Cesare Mainardi, Art Kleiner, *Strategy That Works***

Powerful Execution Tip: In execution, time is the only non-recoverable resource.

While building your HOW, consider putting required funding in place early. As a McKinsey & Company survey[41] noted, firms that actively reallocate capital expenditure across business units achieve an average shareholder return that's 30% higher than the average return of organizations that were slow to shift funds.

In another example, in 2014, CEB reported from its Chief Strategy Officer research that freeing up resources is as important as building commitment cross

---

40 https://hbr.org/2016/01/whos-better-at-strategy-cfos-or-csos
41 http://www.mckinsey.com/insights/strategy/how_to_put_your_money_where_your_strategy_is

the organization when launching a new strategy. Freeing up capacity increased effectiveness and created a 31% improvement in success.

To leverage resources effectively requires reducing the number of ongoing initiatives so everyone is focused on the highest priorities with the right support.

> *Powerful Execution Tip*: For leaders, assessing the capabilities required to achieve Excellence in Execution may create more project work, but consider this is good strategic risk management planning.

8. Make Actions Fun

Providing the right resources and holding people accountable for their commitments can also be enhanced by making work fun!

In an experiment by the car company Volkswagen, leaders demonstrated that people's actions can be changed for the better by making mundane activities fun. For example, in the staircase of a Stockholm subway station, a musical piano was placed near the steps to see if more people would choose the healthier option and take the stairs instead of the escalator. The experiment resulted in 66% more people taking the stairs than usual.[42] A similar experiment was conducted in making it fun to cross on a footbridge rather than cut cross traffic. The bridge was made to squeak as people walked on it, and the flow across the bridge almost doubled as a result.

Excellence in Execution is a serious subject, but it doesn't mean you and your people can't have fun with it. When I travel, I put a rubber chicken in my carry-on luggage in a way that the feet stick out. Seeing it puts a smile on the airport security officer's face, a rare occurrence.

> *Powerful Execution Tip*: To encourage people to take the right action, find ways to make Excellence in Execution easier and fun.

Next, Part Two focuses on making your execution your own. It details the Three Broad Themes of Execution and provides you with the tools, tips and

---

42 https://www.youtube.com/watch?v=2lXh2n0aPyw

templates to ensure your organization knows what to do and how to do it. It also discusses the uncommon practices of organizations that have successfully executed strategy and has designed questions to build your organization's HOW (How Organizations Win). Part Two starts with an introduction to the DBS Bank Case Study and then runs through the section on how Singapore's largest bank achieved Excellence in Execution.

Part Two

MAKING IT YOUR OWN

Overview to DBS Bank

Introduction to DBS Case Study

DBS Bank is a leading financial services group in Asia. It has more than 280 branches across 18 markets and 22,000 employees. Headquartered and listed in Singapore, DBS has a growing presence in the three key Asian axes of growth: Greater China, Southeast Asia and South Asia.

DBS Bank provides a full range of services in Institutional banking, Consumer banking, and Treasury and Markets. As of December 2014, DBS had S$441 billion in total assets, S$9.62 billion in income and a net profit of S$4.05 billion. About 62% of the group income comes from Singapore, 30% from Hong Kong and the rest from Greater China. The remainder comes from South and Southeast Asia and the rest of the world. Assets under management for all of the bank's wealth customers top S$134 billion.

Pre-New CEO (2009)

The year 2009 was an uncertain time in the banking industry at the height of the Global Financial Crisis. The banking industry was undergoing a profound change. Regulators around the world had tightened regulatory standards to remove excesses from riskier aspects of the business and limit speculative activities. Pressure from communities was building to steer banking back to more traditional and genuinely useful activities.

In response, the banking industry underwent a perceptible shift from *expediency* to *values* and from *short-term profit maximization* to *long-term profit sustainability*. Instead of creating banking products that turn toxic, it shifted to ones that facilitated the production of economic goods and services. There were also increasing demands for enhanced reporting so banks could better demonstrate their commitment to corporate governance and responsibility to multiple stakeholders. Other changing trends affecting banks included analytics, technology and customer behavior. In addition, mobile banking was the fastest growing area of contact between customers and the bank.[43]

Prior to Piyush Gupta becoming DBS Bank's CEO in late 2009, the bank was profitable but earnings was impacted by market swings. Further, there was no clarity in the direction that the bank would take following the Global Financial Crisis that had shaken up the financial industry around the world.

Piyush had a positive feeling about DBS from the very beginning, saying, "I felt that DBS had a very good franchise, so the possibilities were very good. On the other hand, if you looked at DBS's history, particularly over the past decade before I joined, it had been very choppy. Fundamentally, the bank had underperformed its potential."

In addition, its Management Information System (MIS) was not rigorous, and although the leaders were busy, they weren't clear what their other colleagues were doing. Missing were no common system for the region, no internal communications, no structured performance appraisals and no standard measurements. Piyush later referred to this as a time to "fix the bank's plumbing."

The bank's strategy targeted Asia as its region of business, but its leaders lacked the discipline to execute that goal. For example, in its acquisition strategy, DBS acquired Kwong On Bank in 1999 and Dao Heng bank in 2001 (both in Hong Kong) but had issues with achieving synergies with them. The bank's board of directors was also hiring its third CEO in four years.

---

43   This summary has the approval of DBS leaders.

In preparation for meeting the board prior to becoming CEO, Piyush conducted an outside-in diagnostic and looked for areas of strengths and opportunities. He identified a strong franchise, a good pedigree and access to capital. Because of the Singapore franchise, the bank was highly liquid and had a good brand reputation around the region. But it had fundamentally underperformed its potential. An opportunity to be a pan-Asian bank was apparent, but what that meant was unclear to people working at DBS Bank.

Board Appoints Piyush Gupta CEO (September 2009)

Piyush hit the ground running and immediately used his first 100 days to meet customers, the leadership team and the employees. It became abundantly clear to those who met him how well he had done his homework before stepping in. He created an immediate positive impression.

During his 100-day deliberation, Piyush identified three key areas to work on:

1. Strategic priorities—Determine which areas the bank should build and which to exit.
2. "Plumbing" of the bank—Several basics to run a regional bank were missing including the MIS as well as operating policies and technologies.
3. Culture challenge—Good things about the bank's culture were being team-orientated and not political. Still, the culture was bureaucratic, decisions were pushed up to the executives and committees, and employees were reluctant to make decisions and challenge the status quo.

After the first three months of in-depth discussions with everyone in the bank's circle, Piyush took his top leaders on a three-day leadership retreat to craft a new strategy and address challenges.

The Design of the Retreat (early 2010)

The 2010 retreat was held on Sentosa, a popular island resort in Singapore. The agenda included these goals:

1. Think hard about the purpose and identity of what the bank wanted to stand for.
2. Create clarity around direction and strategic priorities to achieve a competitive advantage.
3. Identify the purpose of the bank.
4. Build a strong relationship between the CEO and the senior leaders of the bank.
5. Identify the enablers required for change (e.g., risk appetite, support, infrastructure, people and technology).

In Day One of the retreat, DBS's CEO and his leadership team reviewed, analyzed and addressed macro trends and the competitive landscape. Against that backdrop, the participants crafted the strategic statement for the bank. This stated what the bank wanted to do (e.g., identify a niche position where it would focus only on Asia) and what it did not want to do (e.g., not compete as a global bank).

Day Two identified the strategic objectives and priorities by answering two key questions: (1) Where do we want to play? and (2) How do we want to win? Each country's business and product offerings were analyzed and linked to the macro trends. They also discussed the large opportunities in the Hong Kong market as well as 1) the growth markets of China, India and Indonesia, 2) the Transaction banking business, 3) the Small and Medium Enterprise business and 4) the Wealth Management business.

Day Three focused on identifying the enablers for achieving the strategic objectives. This included how to build people talent, culture, infrastructure and technology while creating a holistic view of the customer.

Outcome of Retreat

The strategy that came out of this 2010 retreat covered three main areas:

1. What we want to be—Asian Bank of Choice for the New Asia
2. Nine Strategic Priorities

3. Principal areas of differentiation and competitive advantage—Five Asian Pillars

1. Asian Bank of Choice for the New Asia

Specifically, the strategy identified how DBS could be the Asian Bank of Choice for the New Asia. Not a domestic bank and not an international bank, it would occupy the sweet spot between the two. From that emerged a vision of an Asian bank distinct from local lenders or global players. By specializing in Asia, DBS would have the reach and sophistication to outcompete local lenders and deep Asian insights that distinguished the bank from its global competitors.

"If we did banking the Asian way, then we would be different from the locals and different from the global banks. The sense of strategy is competitive differentiation—how do we position ourselves differently? This created the capacity."
—Piyush

New Asia was a forward-looking statement of what the bank thought Asia was turning out to be—more sophisticated and confident about itself. But the bank also did not want to lose sight of the values that made Asia special.

It was also agreed that DBS had to be strong at home. How could it be known as a strong Asian bank without dominating Singapore?

By 2020, Asia's GDP is expected to double, growing by a projected USD 11.5 trillion. Meanwhile, the U.S. will only have an expected growth by USD 4.6 trillion. This projects that Asia will add 2.5 times new demand from the U.S. during the decade and become a more significant economic driver. If this trajectory is achieved, then by 2020, wealth in Asia will be 17% bigger than the U.S.

Currently, Asia is creating wealth faster than anywhere in the world. A growing middle class and rising numbers of high net worth individuals are changing consumption patterns and creating new markets. Asia is no longer only the factory of the world but an increasingly significant marketplace as domestic consumption becomes a bigger driver of economic growth. These consumers will need customized financial solutions to fund their lifestyle needs and manage their assets.[44]

2. Strategic Priorities

The priorities identified at the retreat were in three areas:

Geographies
1. Entrench its position in Singapore
2. Reposition the Hong Kong franchise
3. Rebalance the geographic mix of the business

Regional businesses
4. Build a leading SME banking business across the region
5. Strengthen the wealth proposition across the region to better serve the increasing number of potential new clients

Enablers
6. Build out the Global Transaction Services (GTS) and the treasury customer business across the region
7. Place customers at the heart of the DBS banking experience
8. Focus on management processes, people and culture
9. Strengthen the technology and infrastructure platform

These priorities then formed the basis of the group's Scorecard.

Woven through the strategy and the bank activities was the differentiator of Banking the Asian Way to define relationships with customers and employees. The strategy also allowed the bank to provide unique Asian insights for its customers and design solutions for them while providing seamless connectivity across a network of key Asian markets.

3. Banking the Asian Way

How the bank would differentiate itself became known as these five Asian pillars:

---

44   Published with the approval from DBS

1. Asian Relationships—We strive to embody the elements of what relationships are about in Asia. We recognize that relationships have swings and roundabouts. We look at relationships holistically, recognizing that not every transaction needs to be profitable in its own right. We stay by our clients through down cycles.

2. Asian Service—Our service ethos is built on the RED motto: being Respectful, Easy to deal with and Dependable, with the humility to serve and the confidence to lead.

3. Asian Insights—We know Asia better; we provide unique Asian insights and create bespoke Asian products. Our customer conversations are underpinned by award-winning research that offers insights into markets and industries in Asia.

4. Asian Innovation—We constantly innovate new ways of banking that are appropriate to our markets as we strive to make banking faster, more intuitive and more interactive.

5. Asian Connectivity—We work in a collaborative manner across geographies, supporting our customers as they expand across Asia.[45]

This strategy was presented to the board of directors for approval. The board backed the leadership team and approved opening up to the challenges such as developing trade in China and new technology infrastructure. The board acknowledged it required a higher risk appetite and greater investment than before.

One week after the 2010 retreat and with the board's approval, DBS Bank launched its new strategy in Shanghai when opening its new office there. This event reflected the bank's new regional focus. Strategies and priorities were shared with the analysts and, as they were executed, the results were linked back to the strategic objectives.

The bank leaders had become clear on what success for DBS would look like, what it would take to achieve the strategic outcomes, how to sequence the outcomes and what would be measured. The new strategy and Piyush's stewardship brought stability and then results. In addition, the launch of the

---

45 Published with the approval from DBS

new strategy gave employees an opportunity to create something different, and they rose to the occasion.

Strategy Execution Steps

In discussions among the leaders on both defining strategy and executing it, they gave *execution* equal emphasis with *strategy* from the start.

"It was important to have a very clear and systematic rollout plan for our strategy."
—Piyush

Piyush strongly believed the implementation of the Asian Bank of Choice for the New Asia started with aligning around the strategy across the whole bank. For the 12 to 24 months that followed, it was the single most important thing he had to do. He consistently repeated the message and constantly linked activities and outcomes back to the strategy.

"Strategy implementation first and foremost to me is alignment. The new strategy in 2010 was not that different. The big difference was in the implementation."
—Sok Hui Chng, CFO, DBS

To initiate executing the strategy required changing the mindset of people in the bank to foster a new way of working. Everyone had to understand the strategy and what it meant to them. To assist in this (and the overall implementation), they branded the strategy the DBS House. It later became known as Piyush's House. The DBS House became the "true north," showing *what* and *how* to participate in the implementation. The stated priorities indicated the *what;* the pillars noted the *how.*

Leaders in each country in the bank's network were asked to develop a plan to align with the House. Within a month, they were to report back to Piyush. By design, the roll-out was unified but not uniform; each country and business unit customized it as required to local conditions without changing its overall purpose.

To ensure corporate governance around the implementation, weekly executive committee (Exco) meetings were held. Every two weeks, the group management committee (GMC) met. Piyush held regular business meetings and visited countries and clients. Periodic reviews were established with every country, business and support unit. Once the leaders had locked in the strategy, they were ready to Create Awareness across the whole bank so people would start taking the right actions to execute that strategy.

Excellence in Execution Challenges
Create Awareness

As a leader, you learn how to:

- Ensure your people understand why the organization needs a new strategy
- Create a sense of urgency
- Inspire and engage people to participate
- Ensure people take the right actions
- Cultivate a supporting network and environment
- Develop clear, constant communication

Language of Excellence in Execution
Over the Wall, Share of Mind, Strategy Story, Inspired to Implement, Mavericks Network

Materials featured in this book are available at www.implementation-hub.com/tools_tips_techniques/excellence-in-execution.

Chapter Eight

Create Awareness

 Video Quiz: Three days after hearing an important message, what percentage can people recall of the message?

The first of the Three Broad Themes to be discussed, Create Awareness, addresses *why* the organization must transform, *what* the new strategy is and *how to* generate a sense of urgency around the new strategy. It also explains *why* and *how* people need to participate.

With people not knowing their own organization's strategy (note Bridges' research[46]) and only one in five people readily adopting it, what happens when leaders go straight to telling people what to do differently? The execution stumbles right from the start.

People need to understand the reasons to transform. By learning what needs to be communicated and customizing presentations to different audiences, leaders can generate a good first impression when introducing the new strategy (something that doesn't always happen).

---

46 http://www.implementation-hub.com/resources/implementation-surveys

> **Without taking the time to consider the best way to share the new strategy during planning, a difficult journey becomes even harder and can lead to a stumble that many organizations never recover from.**

Part of the initial thinking when deciding how to present the new strategy is recognizing people have different preferences. As a light example, what are your preferences?

- Apple or Galaxy phones?
- Working in the morning or at night?
- Tea or coffee?
- Smart or casual attire?
- Work alone or in a group?
- LinkedIn or Facebook?
- Window or aisle seat on the plane?

Just as everyone will answer these questions based on their own preferences, people have their own ways of answering the call to implement a new strategy. Leaders who achieve Excellence in Execution recognize this as they prepare communications during the HOW. They consider how to respond to people's different preferences and strive to create the right first impression.

> **You never get a second chance to start a good execution.**

 Six Common Pitfalls in Creating Awareness

Given that most employees are unable to explain even the broad strokes of their organization's strategy, the current communication approach doesn't work. Here are the most common pitfalls to avoid that I have gathered from my work and research:

Pitfall #1: Relying on town hall meetings and emails

The challenge to Create Awareness requires more than a handful of messages.

When leaders perceive the Create Awareness goal is only to notify everyone about the new strategy, then they believe holding a town hall meeting or email will suffice. In one example, a regional manager of a medical supplier delivered eight two-hour 160-slide presentations around his region. But when someone in a session asked him a question afterward, he replied, "I showed you that in the presentation." In this regional manger's mind, *he had explained the strategy and was done.*

Many leaders are guilty of communicating across too few mediums. They provide too little information and their people don't understand why the organization must transform, so they don't take any new actions.

The aim is not to launch the strategy but to nurture the communications throughout the implementation journey.

Pitfall #2: "Strategy Speak"—Overcomplicating communication

Leaders sometimes overcomplicate what they're saying, making it hard for people to understand even the simplest message. They have a bad habit of using "strategy speak"—saying popular expressions and giving long explanations rather than speaking simply and directly. This has been done on so many occasions, it has even given birth to a game called corporate bingo! In this game, before a leader's presentation, people are given bingo sheets with corporate jargon, and they complete the sheet during the presentation. A 2008 commercial by IBM poked fun at this.[47]

To be effective, leaders communicate the strategy in a way that enables people to understand what's changing. They explain why transformation is needed and clearly state what people should do differently. They avoid using ambiguous terms that blur the objectives and leave people confused about what actions to take.

---

47 https://www.youtube.com/watch?v=ZIxcxfL5jas

Research has found that when people use long, complicated words, listeners assume they themselves are less intelligent than the speaker. That's partly why simplicity is key. The easier it is for listeners to understand what you're saying, the more likely they are to believe it.

"The more technologically advanced our society becomes, the more we need to get back to basic fundamentals of human communication."
—**Angela Ahrendts, Senior VP retail and online stores, Apple**

Pitfall #3: Dumbing down the strategy message

Some leaders dumb down the strategy message too much when sharing it. This is the opposite of Pitfall #2: "Strategy Speak." Leaders leave out key messages, arguments and persuasion points. As a result, people lack relevant information to understand why changing strategy is important and lack a desire to participate. Keeping the strategy message clear and straightforward is different than dumbing down the message. As Albert Einstein said, "If you can't explain it simply, you don't understand it well enough."

Leaders must convey relevant content and translate the strategy into an understandable language that will inspire people to participate.

Pitfall #4: Not reinforcing awareness with actions

The awareness efforts fail if leaders are saying one thing and doing something else. Their words have to be aligned with actions that are reinforced. People in the organizations have to not only *hear* about the transformation from their immediate bosses but *see* them being consistent in their values and actions.

When Meg Whitman took over as CEO of Hewlett Packard (HP), she wanted to encourage a return to the HP Way. One thing she noticed was how the executive leadership was fenced off from the organization. This was communicating the wrong message to the employees. In her April 2013 online post "The Power of Transparent Communication"[48] she commented, "Nothing symbolized this disconnect more than our executive offices and what I called the 'commando fence'—a large fence outfitted in barbed wire surrounding our executive parking lot. The walled offices and military-style fence represented just how far HP had departed from the culture of the company's founders.

"One of the first things I did was tear down the fence and move all of our executives into cubicles. We now walk in the same door as the rest of our employees. This was symbolic of the kind of culture that we wanted to build. And in organizations as large as ours, symbolism actually matters. What you communicate by your actions—the things that are visible to 320,000 people— make a real difference." Whitman ensured that the organization's actions reinforced its communication.

> **"Take time to deliberate, but when the time for action comes, stop thinking and go in."**
> **—Napoléon Bonaparte**

Pitfall #5: Not communicating a message that inspires

When leaders are preparing the strategy execution message, what they base their main message on doesn't typically relate with the majority of people's inspirations. They often talk about market share, client impact and financial performance. With the exception of investment bankers and a few others, most people don't come to work in the morning feeling passionate about adding shareholder value. They simply aren't inspired by this kind of language, so they don't take the new actions required to execute. Rather, they go back to work and keep doing what they were doing. As a result, the execution fails to gain traction.

---

48   https://www.linkedin.com/pulse/20130423170055-71744402-the-importance-of-transparent-communication?trk=mp-reader-card

---

Leaders have to identify the factors that encourage their people to participate and then speak directly to those factors.

Pitfall #6: Discussing the medium before the message

Commonly, leaders struggle to agree on how a message should be disseminated before they agree what should be said and why. Should we create a website? How many pages should it have? How about a video? What about an email from the CEO? These questions are thrown around, but they distract leaders from communicating the right messages through the right medium to the right audience. Leaders first need to identify what they want people to hear *before* they discuss ways to share it.

For example, to communicate the new strategy, the executives of Rolls Royce identified six essential messages and then created storyboards—that is, they translated the strategy and resulting actions into visual images. Then they trained 75 leaders to conduct 4,000 presentations.

"Failure to communicate strategy causes frontline workers to invent their own strategy."
—Anonymous

By overcoming these six pitfalls, you leverage the opportunity of making a good first impression with the strategy launch and moving people *over the wall*.

Over the Wall

This metaphor explains the rationale people need at the start of the execution to understand why they should adopt and participate in the new strategy. Imagine your people standing on one side of a wall (see Figure 8.1). The aim is to assist them to climb over the wall to the other side in their understanding of what's needed. The challenge lies in recognizing what tactics will move them over that wall. This becomes a structured part of the HOW—How Organizations Win.

Figure 8.1

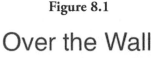

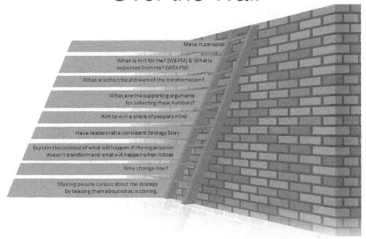

Make it personal

What is in it for me? (WIJ-FM) & What is expected from me? (WEX-FM)

What are the critical drivers of the transformation?

What are the supporting arguments for selecting these numbers?

Aim to win a share of people's mind

Have leaders tell a consistent Strategy Story

Explain the contrast of what will happen if the organization doesn't transform and what will happen when it does

Why change now?

Making people curious about the strategy by teasing them about what is coming

 Nine Tactics for Moving People Over the Wall

The nine tactics are:

1. Make people curious about the strategy by teasing them about what is coming.

This can be done by suggesting what will happen without giving employees the full picture. Like a jigsaw puzzle, the strategy image slowly reveals itself. As David Sibbet, president and founder of The Grove Consultants International, noted, "People are more engaged by things that are suggestive than by things that are crystal clear.[49]" This message can become the fundamental principle for how you design the Biz Case on the Implementation Compass.

> *Powerful Execution Tip*: People are more engaged when they can reach their own conclusions about why the organization must transform on their own. Present the reasons to adopt a new strategy in a way that allows them to reach the right conclusions and take the right actions.

---

49   David Sibbet, Visual Meetings, Wiley & Sons, 2010, p 56.

For example, while working with the Cisco leadership in Europe, we created images that showed the threats to the current business from both "inside/out" and "outside/in" perspectives. The image highlighted the reasons Cisco had to transform. It helped people reach their own conclusions about the change and made it possible for leaders to easily share it with their people.

2. Explain why now.

An ideal time to create a new strategy is when revenue has never been better, sales are strong and customer satisfaction is high. It's easier to craft and execute a new strategy when all is going well. Also, after an organization hits a peak, the only place it can go is down, so leaders need to have a new strategy in place to avoid a decline in business.

When the organization is performing well, it appears illogical to many employees to start transforming it. They question embracing a new strategy when business has never been better. In effect, they hit the wall rather than go over it.

By viewing the situation from 50,000 feet, leaders are responsible for recognizing when it's time to transform and then winning people over by stating why. They explain that although the outlook looks good today, circumstances are changing and the organization needs to transform or be left behind.

3. Contrast what will happen if the organization doesn't transform compared with what will happen when it does.

Saying what will be lost if the organization doesn't transform assists in moving people over the wall. Leaders draw a contrast between what will happen if the organization doesn't transform and what will happen once it executes the new strategy.

Powerful Execution Tip: People's minds are influenced when they understand the compelling reasons to transform.

4. Have the leaders tell a consistent strategy story.

The strategy story can be told in less than five minutes, yet it results in listeners starting to become emotionally and logically attached to the new strategy. It typically includes an image or a strategy map.

In their article "The psychology of change management"[50] Emily Lawson and Colin Price from McKinsey noted that the first of four basic conditions necessary before people will change their behavior is hearing a compelling story. Why? Because people must see the point of the change and agree with it. (The other three points are leaders as role models, having in place reinforcing mechanisms and capability building.) A strategy story explains the following:

- what the transformation involves
- the need to transform now
- the result if we *don't* adopt the new strategy
- the result when we *do* adopt the new strategy
- the benefits of the strategy

5. Aim to win a share of people's mind.

In advertising, it's share of market; in banking, it's share of wallet; in online advertising, it's share of voice; in execution, it's share of mind.

In attempting to capture employees' share of mind, leaders are constantly competing with dozens of messages from a wide range of media surrounding them. They aim to rise above the noise with memorable messaging about *why* the organization has to transform. This requires creativity and consistency in the messaging and is achieved through branding the strategy. (See the side bar on 3X3 and 7X7.)

6. Determine the supporting arguments for the numbers presented.

In making their arguments, leaders need to state up front any assumptions they've made. Doing so will pre-empt any concerns that may arise as they present

---

50   http://www.mckinsey.com/business-functions/organization/our-insights/the-psychology-of-change-management

their case for transformation. Failing to explain their supporting arguments can result in people lacking confidence in the whole execution right from the start.

One execution team found out that, while it was relatively easy to state the cost savings, the proposed increase in revenue proved difficult to explain and was subject to being challenged. Once the leaders clarified their assumptions when calculating the increased revenue, the number of challenges was significantly reduced. Most important, people came away having confidence in the strategy presented.

> *Powerful Execution Tip*: A general rule of thumb is to communicate facts upward in the organization hierarchy and stories downward.

7. Describe the key actions of the execution.

Once leaders have explained the compelling reasons, the strategy story and the numbers, the next step is to describe the key actions for execution and how people can participate. If key actions are missing, then they will likely do nothing, as the following story conveys.

The CEO of a prominent telephone company knew his competitors were closing the gap on customer satisfaction levels. He announced he wanted the rate of customer satisfaction to improve by five percentage points and declared that, if the company could meet this target, everyone on staff would receive a bonus. He also used compelling reasons to make sure people knew the benefits of their participation in the new strategy. Yet at year's end, the customer satisfaction index remained unchanged.

This index failed to go up largely because people didn't know *how* to improve customer satisfaction. The leaders didn't explain the key actions to improve customer experience.

8. For each person, determine what's in it for me (WII-FM) and what's expected from me (WEX-FM).

If you recognize these two terms, you're likely familiar with my previous books. They mean when people hear about a new strategy, one of the first questions they ask is "what's in it for me?" (WII-FM) and "what's expected from me?" (WEX-FM).

Think back over the launch of different strategies you've been part of. Did anyone ever clearly explain how you would be affected, what you needed to do differently and how you should do it? Many launches don't include an explanation of these two terms. As a result, people hear the new strategy and continue working the same way.

It's every leader's responsibility to bridge this gap. Throughout the organization, each person should be approached by an immediate boss who explains how he or she can contribute to the strategy execution.

9. Make explanations personal, not generic.

When you explain the reasons the organization needs to transform, you have to make them personal. Here's why. In an experiment at the University of Oregon, psychologist Paul Slovic tested two groups when asking them to give donations. The first group was told about a starving young girl, the poverty across a continent and the millions of people suffering. The second group was only told about one starving young girl. Which group donated more?

People donated more to save the single girl than to save a continent because it felt personal to them.[51]

These nine tactics move your people to other side of the wall—the execution side.

The following four examples explain how CEOs from the airline, technology postal and vegetable seeds industries started to help their people *over the wall*

Example #1: Jeff Smisek, former CEO of Continental United, shared lessons he learned from the merger of the airlines that saved Continental in the mid-1990s. Referring to the company's business plan called the Go Forward Plan (a short statement of the company objectives on marketing, finance, operations and people), he said, "It's a simple plan, easy to understand no matter where you work in the company. It's one piece of paper that focuses everyone." He told his

---

51   http://journal.sjdm.org/7303a/jdm7303a.htm

people, "If you're doing something and can't track it back to the Go Forward Plan, stop what you're doing and do something else."[52]

Example #2: Former IBM CEO Lou Gerstner told the story that during the IBM transformation of the late 1990s, he constantly referred to the metaphor of Tarzan. He encouraged his leaders to think of leading change as swinging through a jungle and letting go of the vine of the business to grab the vine of the new business they were creating with the threat of hungry lions below and the horizon of success slightly visible through the trees. During the merger process, he also made a point of treating people as he wished to be treated—honestly and directly.

Example #3: Faced with declining postal volumes and a rapidly changing consumer landscape, the Singapore postal service aimed to become the leading eCommerce logistics and communications provider in Asia Pacific. Wolfgang Baier, Group CEO at SingPost, told me he used a football metaphor to translate his strategy of transforming the organization to both mail and eCommerce. This worked well because many of his employees were football fans. They related to the SingPost transformation being like a football team striving to win.

Example #4: When preparing to execute their new strategy in 2017, the CEO of my client East West Seed, Bert van der Feltz, called his top performers from around the world together in 2016, (he calls them the "Trailblazers"). At the start of the meeting Bert asked each of them to share why the previous strategy had not performed to its maximum values. These lessons were then adopted in to the new strategy execution plan to assist employees *over the wall.*

Consider that by the time leaders are ready to launch a new strategy, they are already standing on the other side of the wall. They have been living and breathing it for months or longer. As a result, they've come to understand the compelling reasons to transform and the actions to be taken.

Yet many may have forgotten the emotional and logical experience of going *over the wall* themselves. As a result, they fall short in convincing their people

---

52 http://archive.fortune.com/2011/04/19/news/companies/jeff_smisek_united_continental. fortune/index.htm

why the transformation is necessary. But given that they spent months living and breathing the new strategy, how could they expect employees to have their same level of engagement after only a 45-minute briefing?

Powerful Execution Tip: Understand the transformation from your people's perspective and identify the right tactics to take them *over the wall*.

A common step in moving people *over the wall* is to communicate the reasons to transform. Consider these nine steps when composing the reasons:

 Nine Steps for Writing Down the Reasons to Transform

1. Start by describing why the organization has to transform.
2. State the business issue both emotionally and logically.
3. Describe the opportunity that exists and its urgency.
4. Explain how the strategy addresses both the problem and the opportunity.
5. Summarize how the strategy was selected.
6. Provide the rationale for the strategy execution approach.
7. State both the financial and nonfinancial expected benefits.
8. Explain the WII-FM and WEX-FM.
9. Draw a picture of what the future will look like.

Powerful Execution Tip: To keep your people engaged throughout the journey, as a leader, you have to remain engaged yourself throughout the whole implementation journey.

In 2012, INSEAD conducted a study[53] on why some employees in several hundred organizations understand and accept their company's strategy better than others and move over the wall more quickly. Researchers identified that:

---

53   http://www.insead.edu/facultyresearch/research/details_papers.cfm?id=31134

- 16% of the employees embraced the strategy,
- 71% were not bothered, and
- 13% were resistant to embracing it.

Leaders tend to assume the percentage of people resisting would be higher than 13%, which causes them to design their executions with the wrong focus. The study concluded that greater alignment with the organization strategy comes from employees who experience more:

- Positive job conditions
- Engaged supervisors
- Engaged senior leaders

In addition, it showed an employee's positive relationship with his or her immediate boss is a strong driver for experiencing engagement.

Two Waves of Communicating Through the Implementation Journey

Once people start moving *over the wall*, leaders' top challenges include to consistently provide the right communications. In the 2016 Bridges survey, *poor communication* was voted the top reason execution fails. In fact, it's constantly been in the top five reasons over the years. Leaders know it but aren't significantly improving their communication. This is because they focus mostly on the first wave of communication efforts and considerably less on the second. The two waves are:

- **First Wave**—creating the communication plan, launching the strategy and taking people *over the wall* to Create Awareness.
- **Second Wave**—communicating the right messages and updates over time, and making progress toward achieving the strategic objectives to Build Excellence and Follow Through.

Both waves are essential for building communication bridges among the Create Awareness and Build Excellence and Follow Through phases.

Astonishingly, in many organizations, the Second Wave of Communication is almost nonexistent, which contributes to executions failing. Only when both waves are addressed with the right amount of weight for your organization do people understand and then embrace the strategy. Figure 8.2 reflects the appropriate weight to apply.

Figure 8.2

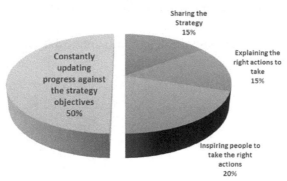

First Wave of Communication

This wave addresses formulating a communication plan and launch of the strategy to Create Awareness.

When leaders see the goal as only sharing the strategy, they are achieving only 15% of the overall communications goal. That's why so many execution efforts struggle from the start. *Sharing the strategy* is only the first step to ensure people become alert to it. The next step involves *understanding what to do differently*.

A massive communications chasm exists between employees being alert to a new strategy and actually knowing the right actions to take. Leaders bridge this chasm by explaining the right actions (15% of the overall communications goal) as they drive and champion the execution itself. Explaining the right actions does not mean telling people what to do (a recipe for failure). Instead, it calls for explaining what needs to happen for the strategy to be executed and then letting people choose the right actions to take.

Next, leaders need to inspire their people to take the right actions (20% of the overall communications goal) with ongoing effort and focus. Just because people know what to do does not mean they will do it, which is explained in more detail in the section Inspiring Your People.

> *Powerful Execution Tip:* It's impossible for leaders to identify all the actions an organization needs to take to execute a strategy. Assist your people to identify what's needed and the right actions to take and then inspire them to act.

When Creating Awareness through communications, you can apply these three useful tools:

- Combine logic and emotion
- 3X3
- 7X7

 ## Combine Logic and Emotion in Your Communications

When initially sharing their strategy, many leaders only communicate logic-based messages supported by statistics. For example, they share the expected financial benefits or impact on the market. To be persuaded to take action, people need both facts *and* emotional considerations. A balance of both is required. Professor Kotter from Harvard Business School put it this way, "Most people won't want to help if you appeal only to logic with numbers and business cases."[54] By addressing both logic and emotions, you target the largest demographic and aim for the highest level of engagement.

> *Powerful Execution Tip:* Adopt both the logical and emotional into Creating Awareness so you can persuade as many people as possible. Share both stories that touch the heart as well as facts that touch the mind.

---

54 John P. Kotter. *Accelerate: Building Strategic Agility for a Faster-Moving World.* Harvard Business Review Press, 2014. p. 24.

3X3 Rule + 7x7 Rule

The human brain has a cognitive bias, which means humans are more likely to believe a familiar statement than a brand new one, even if the familiar statement is wrong! The more people hear it, the more they believe it's true.

Leaders can use this effect to their advantage by identifying three different ways of phrasing the key message into their speeches. They simply make the same argument three times (3X). Please note it's not about repeating the same words; it's about phrasing it in three different ways—3X3.

As the basis of learning, repetition strengthens the connections between neurons that convey information. It's why children who are learning constantly repeat their words.

When communicating, it's important to mix the media used to share messages. *Bricks to Bridges* introduced the 7x7 Rule—a popular practice with clients and in workshops.

The 7X7 Rule refers to marketing a message internally in seven different ways. Using various media helps to ensure people have heard, understood and implemented the message. Different people notice different things every time they see or hear a message, which makes this rule necessary.

> *Powerful Execution Tip*: Create an online portal to encourage people to anonymously ask about the strategy and its execution. Ensure they receive responses from the leadership team within one working day. This quick response reflects the importance of the strategy and acknowledges their involvement.

Janis Foreman and Paul A. Argenti (2005) from UCLA and Amos Tuck School of Business respectively, commented that ". . . although an entire discipline is devoted to the study of organizational strategy, including strategy execution, little attention has been given to the links between communication and strategy."[55]

---

[55] http://link.springer.com/article/10.1057/palgrave.crr.1540253 `

In many organizations, execution fails after the First Wave of Communication, which is centered around the strategy launch. Often, people receive only trickled-down and uncoordinated bits and pieces, leaving them struggling to decipher what's happening. Communication about the execution is allowed to dissipate, and people stop discussing it within a relatively short time.

When people don't understand how to participate in the execution, it delays the rollout, lowers engagement and causes confusion. However, when communication is consistent and effective, it aligns the way individuals think and act, creating a sense of espirit de corps. At the same time, it accelerates the Strategy Cadence.

By improving how you communicate the strategy, you can succeed when many of your competitors fail.

Powerful Execution Tip: To adopt something new requires repetition and intensity. Develop the new skills people require to execute the strategy.

Second Wave of Communication

As the First Wave ripples out, keep the communications alive and focused throughout the implementation journey by sharing the right messages repeatedly through the right medium. Specifically, use the Second Wave to provide progress updates against the strategic objectives while also reporting on the work being done, success stories and lessons learned. This keeps execution on everyone's agenda and reinforces its importance. The Second Wave is a powerful best practice among Excellence in Execution organizations and requires a disciplined effort by leaders.

The Second Wave of communications requires constantly communicating progress against the strategy and its objectives along the implementation journey.

Second Wave of Communication

During the implementation journey's Second Wave, check on these items frequently:

✓ Progress against strategy objectives—This keeps people informed on how they are doing.

✓ What's working and what's not—This creates a learning environment in which successes can be replicated and failures can be eliminated.

✓ Customer feedback—Listening to the voices of your customers includes gathering their feedback on the strategy and sharing its implications.

✓ Progress against the metrics—This provides updates of the execution's analytics.

✓ Share success stories—Doing this keeps people engaged and encourages them to take the right actions.

✓ Work improvements—This requires sharing how some people are changing the way they work to advance the execution.

✓ Milestones achieved—When appropriate, celebrate milestones and small successes.

✓ Strategy deviations—Leaders make changes to the strategy and explain why.

✓ Lessons learned—People share relevant experiences and lessons learned from different business lines.

Silence is a Killer

After the launch, leaders can find themselves polarized into talking about either operations or executions. As they tend to be held more accountable for short-term performance rather than long-term results, the short-term topics dominate the agenda. "Urgent trumps important"—a phrase made popular by the late Stephen Covey—is believed to have evolved from U.S. President Eisenhower's Urgent/Important Principle.[56]

---

56 https://www.mindtools.com/pages/article/newHTE_91.htm

If the communication around the execution is allowed to dissipate in the organization, the silence can be a killer. In a climate of silence, people stop raising concerns, issues and challenges they face. They even fill the communication gap by making things up. Typically, they'll identify actions that defend their silo rather than focus on actions for the good of the whole organization. All this makes the difficult job of execution even tougher. If there's no mention of the new strategy, no updates and no questions about it, people resort to focusing on day-to-day activities. As a result, their execution intentions and actions fall by the wayside, setting up failure. Thus, a balance is required between discussing operations and the execution itself.

> *Powerful Execution Tip*: Six months into your execution, check the balance between "execution" versus "operations" discussions.

A Plan within a Plan

A sub-team from the leadership is assigned to develop a detailed communications plan. This is then presented for discussion, agreement and buy-in to the rest of the leadership team. To assist in this process, Bridges has designed a one-day structured workshop called the Communication Foundation Workshop www.bridgesconsultancy.com/one-page-outlines/commutation-foundation-workshop. This workshop ensures everyone understands the strategy objectives and shares the right messages. It also gives structure to what can be a disorderly discussion. The workshop, conducted during the HOW, also assists in developing the Biz Case and internally branding the strategy.

 ### Communication Foundation Workshop

The one-day onsite Communication Foundation Workshop presents a significant building block to crossing the communication chasm. It involves six to eight leaders, including the communications and strategy director. Participants identify and/or create:

- Communication Statement for the strategy
- Communication objectives of the strategy
- Description of target audience and working environment
- Messages to communicate consistently
- Key messages for the strategy that need to be part of the internal branding of the strategy
- Measures to track the communication of the strategy
- Key tactics, activities and budget

The outcome is a communication plan that articulates a timeline and key messages to be shared with different segments of the organization. Communication measures and 90-day tactics are established and internal branding developed. These elements ensure the right first impression is formed at the launch and that people will see and hear consistent messages that inspire them.

Internal Branding of the Strategy

After completing the Communication Foundation Workshop, participants in the organization are then able to brand the strategy internally. The internal branding provides a powerful way to explain both the logic and emotional reasons for the new strategy. At the same time, it captures the essence in an image and often includes a memorable tagline. It leverages visual communications and assists in translating the purpose of the strategy and can include using charts, story boards, videos that present numbers and show relevant data graphically. For example, at DBS Bank, leaders created the DBS House image to communicate the strategy with the whole organization.

Research has revealed that 72 hours after hearing a message *in only words*, people can only recall 10% of it. *This is the answer to the video quiz.*

When words and images are combined, the recall potentially jumps to 65% from 10% for words only. Think of Nike's "swoosh" with its "Just Do It" tagline. Similarly, developing a tagline for your new strategy requires aligning it to other communication media. In part, the Nike branding works well because it's backed by a campaign featuring star athletes to reinforce a belief in product excellence.

In addition, psychological tests have revealed that statements shown *with* images are more believable than words only, even if the two are unrelated.

The more complicated the strategy, the more important it is to make it easily understood by people so they can act on it.

As an example of branding, one of Bridges' clients in India was rolling out the concept of sustainability across the whole organization in 36 countries. The initial branding exercise revealed no common understanding of the word "sustainability." Most people didn't know what the word meant and therefore didn't see why the businesses should adopt it. Participating leaders were led through our Communication Foundation Workshop to understand the challenges, set their communication goals and then brand their strategy. At the workshop, we created this tagline to explain sustainability: *Think About Tomorrow, Today!* It inspires people to care about the future by taking the right actions now.

In tandem with developing the tagline was branding the strategy. This included different images that showed what sustainability meant to people and the organization itself. For the leaders, we initially focused on how sustainability not only supported their business but added value. For the employees, we focused on 12 actions they could take every day to participate in sustainability. This led to a successful launch across multiple countries.

Part of the success of rolling out the sustainability strategy was carefully selecting the right words without using jargon such as "future proofing" or "responsible stewardship." To achieve this, we used the "grandma test"—that is, would your grandma understand the strategy when you explain it to her?

Powerful Execution Tip: Try the grandma test to make sure you are being understood and avoiding jargon. Does your grandma understand what the strategy is when you explain it to her?

Developing a communication plan with both a First and Second Wave ensures a coherent, consistent approach throughout the implementation journey. As a result, employees are not only motivated but inspired to participate.

Where the Buck Stops for the Second Wave

To ensure the right messages are being communicated at the right time through the right media, a powerful technique is to assign the responsibility of the Second Wave to a senior leader, taking up to one sixth of his or her time. Choose someone who has direct access to the CEO as well as having credibility among peers and organizational knowledge and influence.

To Create Awareness, aim to achieve the right balance for communicating inside your organization. Make sure the plan has the right structure and approach as part of the HOW—a plan within a plan—and focusing on inspiring people.

Inspiration versus Motivation

Organizations achieving Excellence in Execution distinguish themselves by their people being inspired and engaged to take the right actions. *Inspiration* is the goal, not motivation.

**"Instead of motivation, look for inspiration.
Inspiration comes from the same word as spirit.
When you are inspired, the spirit moves you."
—Deepak Chopra**

Employees who attend a strategy presentation may be *motivated* at the end of it but not necessarily *inspired*. The word "inspiration" means to be in spirit, to *breathe life into* something. When people are tuned into their spirits, they are drawn to perform their best.

**Leaders must inspire their people to
breathe life into the strategy execution.**

Leaders aim to generate in their people a sense of urgency and purpose that engages them to take the right actions on their own accord over time. However, most strategy presentations only result in motivating people—a quality that has a short-term fuse. In comparison, inspiration is a stronger emotion that lasts significantly longer than motivation.

"Great companies don't hire skilled people and motivate them; they hire already motivated people and inspire them."
—Simon Sinek

Researchers Eric Garton and Michael C. Mankins said, "It would take two and a quarter satisfied employees to generate the same output as one inspired employee."[57] Additional research[58] revealed that inspired people are more creative, robust and targeted in their work.

Nancy J. Adler, Ph.D., S. Bronfman Chair of Management at the Desautels Faculty of Management at McGill University, gave insights in her article "The Arts & Leadership: Now That We Can Do Anything, What Will We Do." She wrote, "Whereas 20th-century managerial frameworks focused primarily on motivation, often attempting to identify sets of rewards and punishment that would inspire workers to produce more, 21st-century leaders know that such motivation is not enough. The leadership challenge today is to inspire people, not simply to motivate them."[59]

How to Inspire Your People

Leaders may attempt to push people toward a desired result through incentives and "rewards and punishment" (as Dr. Adler stated). But although this might have worked in the past for short-term goals, it doesn't work for long-term strategy execution.

---

57   https://hbr.org/2015/12/engaging-your-employees-is-good-but-dont-stop-there
58   http://psycnet.apa.org/journals/gpr/13/3/242
59   http://citeseerx.ist.psu.edu/viewdoc/
      summary;jsessionid=EE400815F9493BD54218D32B283FFE43?doi=10.1.1.505.8017

**Excellence in Execution is achieved by people being inspired
and engaged throughout the implementation journey.**

In this rapidly changing world of people being self-directed, the old model of *control* is being replaced by *inspire*. That means when preparing to Create Awareness, first identify which factors will inspire your people and then address those factors.

One is people feeling the new strategy is personal to them. Piyush Gupta, the CEO of DBS Bank in Singapore, believed that to engage his people, he needed to shake hands with almost every one of the 17,000 people (at that time) in his organization. As he did, he personally invited each of them to participate in the execution.[60]

In other examples, Starbucks CEO Howard Schultz has inspired his people by treating them with dignity and respect. Sir Richard Branson has expressed passion for team members by giving them all of the tools they need to elevate customer service within the numerous companies he owns.

 Inspiring Your People

Ask yourself these questions about how to inspire your people:

✓ **Have you shared the passion around the strategy's potential?**—As a leader, you emerge from crafting the strategy feeling excited about the new opportunities. Transfer that excitement to your people. Become a "state inducer," someone who induces his or her state of mind on others.

✓ **Have you discussed peoples' ideas and thoughts on the strategy?**— Sharing the passion is not enough to inspire. Also listen and discuss the new strategy with your people.

---

60   View Piyush sharing this message: http://www.implementation-hub.com/tools_tips_
techniques/videos/piyush-gupta-chief-executive-officer-and-director-dbs-group

✓ **Have you provided the new skills?**—A new strategy means doing things differently and often using new skills. People feel inspired when given the chance to do so.

✓ **Ask your employees "what can you do to participate in the execution?"**—Keep asking this question. The answers provide guidance and feedback throughout the journey.

✓ **Have you drawn a line of sight between actions and their impact?**—There must be a clear line of sight between the actions the people are taking and the effect they have. You can achieve this by having the right measures in place. Measures demonstrate the impact and provide feedback on performance every two weeks.

✓ **Have you eliminated roadblocks?**—During the implementation journey, various obstacles or roadblocks require you to intervene. Aim to resolve them quickly.

✓ **Have you a "to-stop" list?**—Empower people to abolish projects and processes that no longer add value under the direction of the new strategy.

✓ **Have you aligned reinforcements?**—People must feel they're being recognized for their efforts. Additional work by employees to execute the strategy requires additional work by leaders to reinforce the right actions. Effective leaders offer support at critical moments.

✓ **Have you assisted people to believe in themselves?**—During every execution, people experience good days and bad days. Be present in support of your people, helping them believe in themselves as they work through their tasks.

✓ **Have you built in integrity?**—Leaders build integrity by driving and championing the strategy and doing what they say they will do.

✓ **Are you approachable?**—Be available to discuss the execution and show how you are fair and encouraging.

✓ **Do you treasure your people?**—A leader is only a leader when followers are involved. Without them, it's just a guy out for a walk. Make sure you demonstrate sincere appreciation.

Powerful Execution Tip: Inspire people by putting purpose into their work.

In his excellent book *Start With Why*, Simon Sinek stated, "There are only two ways to influence human behavior: you can manipulate it or you can inspire it."[61] Once people are inspired, then a greater chance of being engaged is possible. Don't be like the CEO who was asked how many people work in his organization. He replied, "About half of them!"

From Inspiration to Engagement

Achieving Excellence in Execution and inspiring your people requires nurturing an increased number of engaged employees. Well-publicized benefits of having engaged employees include higher retention, better performance and more innovation. It's happening when employees take personal responsibility to make things happen.

Inspiration is a stepping stone toward engagement. Employees can be inspired but not engaged, yet if they're engaged, they are also inspired.

Engaged employees have developed a deep connection and level of commitment with the organization. That makes them strong contributors to the execution.

As Susan LaMotte wrote in a 2015 *HBR* article "Employee Engagement Depends on What Happens Outside of the Office," "Companies spend over $720 million each year on employee engagement, and that's projected to rise to over $1.5 billion. And yet, employee engagement is at record lows—13% according to perennial engagement survey leader Gallup."[62]

Gallup also estimated that actively disengaged employees cost U.S. businesses between $450 billion to $550 billion each year in lost productivity. "They are more likely to steal from their companies, negatively influence their co-workers, miss workdays, and drive customers away."[63]

---

61   http://www.goodreads.com/quotes/727763
62   https://hbr.org/2015/01/employee-engagement-depends-on-what-happens-outside-of-the-office
63   http://www.gallup.com/businessjournal/162953/tackle-employees-stagnating-engagement.aspx

In Singapore, Gallop estimated that, "actively disengaged workers penalize Singapore's economic performance, costing between $4.9 and $6.7 billion annually."[64]

KPMG stated in "The real value of engaged employees" that "The level of engagement will positively or negatively influence their willingness to go the extra mile at work, innovate and assist a company in reaching the corporate or unit strategy."[65]

Excellence in Execution requires people to go the extra mile.

An interesting claim by the Institute of Employment Studies[66] is that "Engagement levels decline as employees get older—until they reach the oldest group (60 plus), where levels suddenly rise and show this oldest group to be the most engaged of all." It also showed that "engagement levels decline as length of service increases."[67]

The financial benefit of engaged employees has been recorded in these ways:

- New Century Financial Corporation identified that account executives in the wholesale division who were actively disengaged produced 28% less revenue than their colleagues who were engaged. Furthermore, those not engaged generated 23% less revenue than their engaged counterparts.
- As Gallup found, companies that increase their number of talented managers and double the rate of engaged employees achieve, on average, 147% higher earnings per share than their competitors.[68]
- A frequently quoted 2006 Gallup survey involving almost 24,000 organizations compared financial performance with engagement scores. The results were:

---

64   http://www.gallup.com/businessjournal/1207/Disengaged-Employees-Cost-Singapore-49-Billion.aspx?g_source=position4&g_medium=related&g_campaign=tiles

65   https://www.kpmg.com/US/en/IssuesAndInsights/ArticlesPublications/Documents/real-value-of-engaged-employees.pdf

66   http://www.employment-studies.co.uk/report-summaries/report-summary-drivers-employee-engagement

67   Ibid.

68   http://www.gallup.com/businessjournal/167975/why-great-managers-rare.aspx

- o Engagement scores in the top quartile averaged 12% higher customer advocacy, 18% higher productivity and 12% higher profitability than in the bottom quartile.
- o Engagement scores in the bottom quartile averaged 31% to 51% more employee turnover, 51% more inventory shrinkage and 62% more accidents than in the top quartile.
- The Department of Business & Innovation Skills in the U.K. revealed that organizations with a highly engaged workforce experience a 19.2% growth in operating income over a 12-month period.[69]
- Standard Chartered Bank found that branches with a statistically significant increase in levels of employee engagement had a 16% higher profit margin growth than branches with decreased levels of employee engagement.[70]

**Without having engaged people to execute
the strategy, the implementation will fail.**

Three Common Questions

In Create Awareness, you are moving your people over the wall, communicating in two waves, leveraging a communication plan, and inspiring and engaging your people. There are three common questions I often hear different leaders ask.

1. Should we involve our employees in crafting the strategy?
2. How much of the strategy details do we share with employees?
3. How do we manage people who resist the transformation?

1. To Involve Employees in Crafting the Strategy or Not?

The answer to the first common question evokes two schools of thought. The first argues that a leader's responsibility is to craft the strategy and then ensure

69 http://webarchive.nationalarchives.gov.U.K./20140404151146/http://www.bis.gov.U.K./files/file52752.pdf
70 https://www.officevibe.com/blog/employee-engagement-benefits

it's executed. The other argues that to ensure engagement and participation from people, leaders should give people a voice early in the crafting process. When employees are included in the planning, their willingness, commitment, creativity and responsibility, they argue, are higher than when they aren't included. As Facebook's CEO Mark Zuckerberg stated, "When you give everyone a voice and give people power, the system usually ends up in a really good place."[71]

The answers depend on HOW you make the strategy and the execution your own. It also depends on your culture, environment and business situation. For example, a business in crisis that operates with a Fast Strategy Cadence doesn't have the luxury of time to get people involved, whereas one with a Slow Strategy Cadence does. You decide based on your organization's situation.

2. To Share or Not to Share? That is the Question.

Some leaders are concerned that if they share too much information about a new strategy especially at the start, then it will be leaked to their competitors. Others argue that the more people are informed, the greater the probability they will take the right actions.

In my experience, it's better to share than not. Even if competitors know about your strategy, *knowing* it and *being able to adopt* it are entirely different.

As an example, while I was working with a CEO of a leading organization in Qatar, we debated this point as we prepared to roll out the organization's strategy. I argued that everyone must know the strategy so they become aware of it and can start taking the right actions. The more the organization communicated about the strategy, the less the resistance would be to executing it. A greater number of right actions would result.

Still, this CEO had deep concerns about competitors acquiring the details. So he restricted the communications, informing his leaders and communications people to share only top-level information. Although we successfully achieved the strategy objectives, this organization had to invest time and money in additional activities to explain the new strategy.

---

71   http://www.brainyquote.com/quotes/quotes/m/markzucker412425.html

---

**By the time your competitors have viewed your
strategy and reacted to it, you have already embarked
on your execution. They are playing catch up.**

Jeff Immelt, CEO of GE, published an overview of the company's strategy in its 2005 annual report. When asked by a writer for the *Harvard Business Review* if he wasn't concerned about the competition seeing it, he replied, "GE has not been secretive about the elements of its strategy; they were spelled out in its 2005 annual report. That's because the payoff is not in the diagram but in the doing."[72]

Roger Connors and Tom Smith, who wrote *The Oz Principle,* claim that nine out of 10 leadership teams cannot describe with complete alignment the key results their organization need to achieve. If an organization's top leaders aren't in agreement, how can alignment across the whole organization be expected when no shared communication is taking place?

Powerful Execution Tip: **Less is more** does not apply to communications. To bridge the communication chasm, leaders need to share more, not less.

3. How Do We Manage People who Resist the Transformation?

A flaw in the essence of this third common question occurs when leaders believe most people *resist* adopting and executing a new strategy. Yet, this is not true when it's communicated correctly.

Author Peter Senge framed it well when he said, "People don't resist change. They resist being changed." From my research since 2004 when I first published in *Bricks to Bridges*, I discovered that people respond in one of four ways. (The name Bridges uses for the corresponding group is noted in parentheses.)

1. Indifference (Groupies)
2. Resistance (Saboteurs)
3. Doubt (Double Agents)
4. Support (Mavericks)

---

72   https://hbr.org/2006/06/growth-as-a-process

1. Indifference (Groupies)

The majority of employees—60% of them—sit on the fence. They neither support the execution nor oppose it. Easygoing by nature, they see their job as just a job. They don't seek the spotlight or vie for promotions.

Typically, these fence-sitters arrive at 9:00 am and depart at 6:00 pm. In between, they do their work. They don't volunteer for additional work, but they don't actively resist transformation, either. They like the safety they find in numbers. Based on these characteristics, I call them Groupies.

2. Resistance (Saboteurs)

Within an organization, 18% of people actively resist transformation. These resisters tend to complain about anything and everything. They badmouth the execution behind leaders' backs. They try to convince others this strategy is just another management fad. They even see the new strategy as a threat. Based on these characteristics, they're called Saboteurs.

If their views win out, the whole execution fails. These individuals can make choices or take actions that could damage the organization's new strategy. To deal with them, you either move them over to your view or move them out.

Today, organizations are transforming more often than at any other time in history. As a result, people are also being asked to execute more frequently. Some are willing and others struggle, depending on what's being asked. Organizations can no longer afford to carry people who don't engage in the new strategy, and leaders need to take corrective action. As Steve Jobs said, "It's painful when you have some people who are not the best people in the world and you have to get rid of them; but I have found that my job has been exactly that—to get rid of some people who didn't measure up and I've always tried to do it in a humane way. But nonetheless it has to be done and it's never fun."[73]

3. Doubt (Double Agents)

These approximate 2% of employees are not easy to spot because they are hidden among the Saboteurs. They have seen attempts to transform before and

---

73   http://www.itworld.com/article/2735412/it-management/steve-jobs-interview--one-on-one-in-1995.html?page=2

think, "Most of them fail, so why engage?" However, they are very important. Although they initially resist, they can become Mavericks over time. Based on these characteristics, they're called Double Agents.

Double Agents start out acting like Saboteurs, but once they're convinced this execution will succeed, they come on board and transform into your top supporters, driving the execution with full engagement.

> **"During a time of organization transition, we frequently see people at every level playing not to lose rather than playing to win."**
> **—Roger Connors and Tom Smith,**
> ***Change the Culture, Change the Game***

4. Support (Mavericks)

The remaining 20% are those who welcome the transformation, embrace it and willingly support it. These early adopters drive the execution as top talents who are enthusiastic and optimistic about the transformation. Based on these characteristics, they're called Mavericks. Excellence in Execution lives or dies with Mavericks.

Powerful Execution Tip: Create the time to sit down and talk with people, especially the main supporters of transformation.

Of the four groups, Saboteurs make the most noise and can lead others to wrongly conclude that most people resist transformation. While Groupies keep quiet because they don't want to draw attention to themselves, Mavericks get on with the work at hand. As Tsun-yan Hsieh and Sara Yaks from McKinsey claim in their article "Leadership as the starting point of strategy,"[74] only 3% to 5% of employees throughout the whole organization can deliver breakthroughs in performance. These are some of the Mavericks.

---

74 http://www.mckinsey.com/global-themes/leadership/leadership-as-the-starting-point-of-strategy

In strategy execution, if leaders target engagement of their people based on the belief that most people resist transformation, they risk developing the wrong approach. Instead, they must actively support the people who support the execution—the Groupies and the Mavericks—by creating a network among them. I call it the Mavericks Network. Excellence in Execution requires input from the strategy execution ambassadors—Mavericks—who feel enthusiastic about the future of the organization. Today, more than ever before, Mavericks are needed throughout the organization.

To support Mavericks, leaders need to create the right conditions for them to thrive. They can do that by bringing like-minded people together. The resulting *network* creates easy communication between them and sets up an ecosystem that encourages them.

Powerful Execution Tip: Mavericks can be anywhere in the organization and at any level, so take the time to identify and cultivate their support.

 Creating a Mavericks Network

To create a Mavericks Network in your organization, consider doing these seven things:

1. Create an email group that people can only join when they receive an invitation from the CEO.
2. Provide training in the skills needed to execute (for example, attend Bridge's Masterclass[75]).
3. Once a quarter, bring Mavericks together on conference calls to discuss challenges, best practices, stories, 90-day achievements and lessons learned.
4. Once a year, hold a Mavericks conference when they come together, discuss progress and meet other Mavericks.

---

75 http://www.implementation-hub.com/tools_tips_techniques/articles/masterclass-h.o.w.-to-achieve-excellence-in-execution-avoid-the-most-common

5. Include the fact that being a Maverick increases their opportunity for promotion.
6. Create the "Best of the Best Maverick" award.
7. Integrate Mavericks' performances into the annual bonus plan.

Julie Battilana and Tiziana Casciaro, who have worked in this area, stated in their article "The Network Secretes of Great Change Agents"[76] that:

- Change agents (referring to Mavericks) are in the center of an organization's informal network regardless of their position or title.
- Change agents (Mavericks) who bridge disconnected groups were more effective at implementing dramatic reforms than others. Those with cohesive networks were better at instituting minor changes.
- Being close to fence-sitters (referring to Groupies) was always beneficial. However, having close relationships with resisters (referring to Saboteurs) was a double-edged sword: Such ties helped change agents push through minor initiatives but hindered major change attempts.

In Excellence in Execution organizations, not only are Mavericks Networks created, but people in them are regarded as assets. In a few leading organizations around the world, people are captured as an asset on the balance sheet and not a cost on the profit and loss statement.

When you create the Mavericks Network and recognize the value from inspired and engaged employees, you evaluate your people as an asset and not a cost.

Since 2008, Infosys in India is a rare organization that marks its people as assets on the balance sheet. It adopted the Lev Schwartz human resources accounting model to calculate its people's collective worth. (The model is based on human capital theory that recognizes human capital as one of several forms of

---

76   https://hbr.org/2013/07/the-network-secrets-of-great-change-agents

holding wealth for a business enterprise, such as money, securities and physical capital. In this model of accounting, human capital is treated like other forms of earning assets and thus is an important factor explaining and predicting the future economic growth of the company.[77])

When the strategy execution falls into place, in effect, people feel they have a greater purpose. It drives them to want to take the right actions and be part of the organization.

In general, people want purpose in their lives, and executing a new strategy presents the opportunity to find a greater purpose. The need to Create Awareness typically comes before the ability to Build Excellence.

---

77 http://www.scribd.com/doc/38460535/Lev-Schwartz-Model#scribd

───── *Chapter Nine* ─────

Questions to Build HOW (Part One)

The designed questions that follow are intended to provoke discussion about the Create Awareness phase and initiate building the execution plan. The comments in italics are included to reinforce the key messages.

To Create Awareness, leaders spread a sense of urgency throughout the organization to adopt and execute a new strategy. They confer both emotional and logical reasons to appeal to both people's hearts and minds. This involves first explaining *why* and then *how* the organization needs to transform. To sustain the initial energy from the strategy launch requires constant communication throughout the implementation journey.

HOW Questions to Create Awareness
When first discussing the HOW during the planning, start by asking these questions:

1. How do leaders currently explain the strategy?—*In a workshop I have each leader individually write the key points of the strategy on an index card. This is followed by discussing those points with a partner and then sharing with everyone in the room so everyone can help make the strategy congruent.*

2. Why has execution failed in the organization before (if it has)?—*The objective is to learn from past mistakes and not to repeat them.*

3. What needs to happen differently to achieve Excellence in Execution?—*This leverages starting to think about and then adopting a different approach.*

4. What is the organization's appetite for transformation?

5. What is the most important initial message of the new strategy that needs to be shared with the whole organization?—*This ensures a consistent message throughout.*

6. As leaders, are we communicating the strategy in a straightforward way that enables people to understand what's changing?—*This is answered by asking frontline people what the new strategy is and why it's important.*

7. What are the main reasons for people to adopt it?—*This starts to clarify the "why."*

8. What is expected from people in the execution?—*This starts to clarify the "what."*

9. What's the most meaningful way to start communicating key messages that will create a good first impression?—*Consider the forms of communication that work best in your organization.*

10. What needs to done by the leaders to drive and champion the execution? *It's important for leaders to understand their role in the execution.*

11. How can leaders guide people to take the right actions?—*It takes discipline from the leaders to ensure that both the day-to-day operations and the strategy execution are being discussed and acted on.*

In Create Awareness, part of the initial goal involves moving people *over the wall*. To do this, ask these questions:

12. What will make people curious about the new strategy? *Consider how you can tease them into it as people like to reach conclusions on their own.*

13. Why must the organization transform immediately? *Create a sense of urgency.*

14. What will happen if we do transform, and what will happen if we don't?—*By asking this two-part question, leaders leverage the power of contrast.*

15. What is the strategy story?—*Leaders need to tell a consistent story about the strategy to gain cooperation among people throughout the organization.*

16. What facts and figures are being shared? *Some employees need to see the numbers.*

17. What are the supporting arguments for the facts and figures being shared? *By sharing, you demonstrate the detailed thinking and reduce the number of discussions.*

18. What are the critical actions of the execution? *What key actions do you need people to take?*

19. What's the WII-FM (What's In It for Me) for employees?

20. What's the WEX-FM (What's Expected from Me) for employees?

21. How can the message be made personal to have more impact and relevance?

Plan the Two Waves of Communication. The First Wave addresses creating the communication plan and launching the strategy. The Second Wave continues to drive employees to take the right actions, keeps the execution on people's agenda and keeps them updated on the progress of the execution. Leaders can sustain the communication by asking these questions:

22. How is progress toward achieving the strategy objectives shared?

23. What's working well?

24. What's not working well?

25. What significant customer feedback needs to be shared?

26. What is the performance against the key measures?
27. What success stories can be shared?
28. What work improvements have been noticed? *Encourage employees to share early successful changes.*
29. What milestones have been achieved?
30. Have there been any strategy deviations and what were they?
31. What lessons have been learned?

To develop a communication plan, a sub-team of the leadership group can go through a one-day facilitated workshop (such as Bridges' Communication Foundation Workshop, visit www.bridgesconsultancy.com/one-page-outlines/commutation-foundation-workshop) and receive guidance.

Communication-related questions to ask are:

32. What does the communication need to achieve?
33. What are the organization's strengths and weaknesses in communicating?
34. Who needs to be influenced the most? *Which group of employees has the most impact on the new strategy?*
35. Who makes up the segmented audiences? *Consider all the different groups of employees and rank them on how influential they are to the execution.*
36. What is the specific message for each audience? *The message will be consistent and it varies as you move down the ranking.*
37. How does the organization's current culture influence the strategy execution?
38. What are the Critical Success Factors (CSF) for the communication plan to succeed?
39. How will you know when the organization has achieved its communication objectives?
40. What tactics and activities must be phased in to achieve the objectives across all segmented audiences?
41. What budget is required?
42. How is the strategy branded so it's easily understood?

Developing the communication plan as part of the HOW ensures the organization goes beyond the initial fanfare.

Adopting two waves of communications ensures a coherent, consistent approach over the whole implementation journey and starts to inspire employees to adopt the execution.

The aim for leaders is not to motivate their employees but to inspire them— to breathe life into the execution. This is partly achieved by addressing how individuals can connect to the new strategy and what they can do within their area of responsibility to participate in its execution. Employees need to not only understand the strategy and how to adopt it; they also need to be inspired by their leaders.

To inspire people, ask these questions:

43. How can excitement from the leadership team be transferred to the employees carrying out the execution?
44. What platforms can be created to listen to people as they participate in the execution? *Consider setting up focus groups or chat rooms on the intranet or mobile phone groups or Facebook-invited group discussions.*
45. How will people see the impact of their contribution? *People feel inspired when they can see how their efforts contribute to the strategy.*
46. Do people have the right skills to execute the strategy? *Identify what new skills employees need to take the new actions.*
47. Are people empowered to make the required changes? If not what needs to happen?
48. Do people feel supported and recognized?
49. Are the leaders building integrity by doing what they said they would do?
50. Are the leaders approachable to discuss the new direction and the challenges it will face?

Inspiration leads to engagement. Without it, the execution fails. To build engagement among your people, ask these questions:

51. How will you create the right conditions for action? *Consider what the right environment is within the organization to drive the right actions.*
52. What resources are required?
53. Have the resources been budgeted for?
54. What training is required?
55. How will it be provided? *Consider if, for example, the leaders will conduct the training to demonstrate commitment to the importance of the new strategy.*
56. How will you provide feedback to employees about their contribution?

Engaged employees develop a deeper connection and level of commitment within the organization than those who aren't engaged. They feel invested in the execution and go the extra mile.

The Mavericks (the most engaged employees) need to be supported, which can be done by forming a Mavericks Network. Ask these questions pertaining to the Mavericks:

57. How has your calendar changed to allow more time to communicate the strategy?
58. How can leaders support the employees who most support the execution? *Leaders are dependent on this group for success.*
59. How does the Network support and further encourage Mavericks?

These three common questions can appear at any time during Create Awareness for leaders to discuss:

60. To increase engagement in the execution, should employees be included in the planning of the strategy?
61. How much of the strategy details should leaders share with employees?
62. How should leaders manage people who resist the transformation?
63. What are your organizations hurdles to strategy execution?

This series of questions continues following the Build Excellence and Follow Through sections.

―――― *Chapter Ten* ――――

DBS Creates Awareness

*T*o Create Awareness across DBS, the bank recognized the need to internally brand the strategy. The DBS House image was established for that purpose. On only one page, the image explained the bank's mission, its strategic priorities and its PRIDE! values. It also assisted in explaining to employees what "Banking the Asian Way" meant and translating the strategy into actions for every part of the business. See Figure 10.1.

It was essential for everyone to understand what the bank wanted to do: How could they contribute? Why were they doing it? What was in it for them? The DBS House became an easy reference point for people internally.

At the launch, many employees were unsure how the bank with a strong presence only in Singapore and Hong Kong could truly become an Asian bank. It was communicated that an Asian bank was not only a geographical position but also a different style of banking.

The Asian Service pillar was understood at the start with bank leaders using the expression *Asian Service is about the confidence to lead and the humility to serve.*

Figure 10.1.

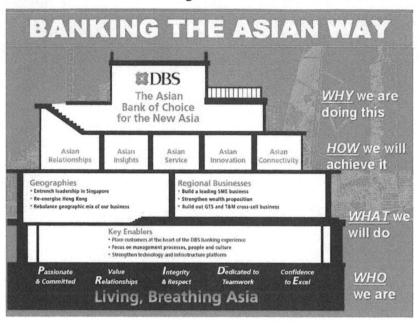

For the first three months of the strategy launch, Piyush and the senior leaders conducted town halls (which became a quarterly event) and attended off-sites to explain the new strategy and why it was important. The leadership team also recognized the need for constant communication to align everyone in the bank to the new strategy. For the next 12 to 24 months, this was the single most important thing Piyush did.

"In those 12, maybe 24, months, it was perhaps
the single most important thing I did—just getting
people aligned to whatever it is we wanted to do."
—Piyush

He continued to invest his time in reinforcing the DBS House. To ensure internalization, Piyush was involved in various meetings and more than 20 strategic workshops across businesses, geographies and support functions.

> **"Messaging is important but just by telling people
> what you want to become does not change them."**
> **—Piyush**

To encourage two-way communication with the CEO and others throughout the bank, a forum called "Ask Piyush" was set up and conducted anonymously over the intranet. To respond to questions asked, Piyush hosted live chats and open forums. These forums created regular and consistent updates on strategy so employees could understand the bigger picture and how each of their roles contributes to the organization's goals. Through this forum, employees realized their feedback was being heard because their comments led to changes in policies and practices.

Piyush also started a blog in 2014 called "RatedPG" (PG for his initials) to share key messages. "Bank Notes" were issued weekly to provide the latest news and results. An internal newspaper called *The Asian Financial Times* also provided a visual reference of the bank's five-year goals.

> **"Communications happen every quarter like clockwork.
> First there will be a board meeting, then the next day
> would be a press release, followed by an investor
> briefing, and followed by employee town halls. Then
> after the town hall, the department heads will take some
> parts of Piyush's presentation and do a session with
> their teams, and their unit heads will communicate on to
> their teams. This is just to make sure that the message
> gets through and everybody understands it."**
> **—Lee Yan Hong, Head of Group Human Resources**

The bank leaders strongly believed in consistent, clear, open communication to enable employees to understand the strategy and their roles related to the bank's execution. Piyush and the senior leaders ensured a consistency of internal messages across the group. Country, functional and department heads also engaged people through channels such as informal lunches, networking sessions and teambuilding workshops.

Piyush had observed that most people in the bank didn't report to his 20 one downs but rather to his two downs. So to ensure the new strategy was shared and then adopted by all, he formed the MC2 (Management Committee 2). This included the top 200 to 250 leaders and talent in the bank. They became the ambassadors of the strategy.

Today, the MC2 continues to meet once a year to discuss and update the company's strategic activities. More than 300 strategy ambassadors are assigned to reinforce key messages. (This became the bank's Mavericks Network—a term discussed in Chapter Eight.) A quarterly call also takes place as a forum for the MC2 to further drive alignment of the group's strategic agenda.

The leaders recognized the importance its people played in execution of the DBS House, so they invested heavily in them. This approach echoed the overall goal of creating an enjoyable good working environment for the right people. It was also reflected through the organization's transformation and investment in real estate in every country. Piyush strived to work with current employees and only brought in new people when required.

"We focused hard on the people agenda."
—Piyush

The employee survey, Gallup Q12, was a good measure of their investment in their people. At the end of 2010, this survey identified that employees did not know what they were supposed to do. Also, the bank had no performance appraisal system in place, which is an essential part of the execution. A performance appraisal provides feedback to people about what the goals are, what to focus on and what they will be rewarded for.

The speed at which the teams addressed the issues identified in the Gallup Q12 reflected their bias for action, the urgency of the new strategy and the leaders' commitment to their people. In September 2011, for example, it was agreed that a formal performance appraisal system was necessary. Two months later in November, a performance review system got approved and by February 2012, the system was launched across all six countries. Today, there is 95% participation rate in the Gallup Q12. (The discrepancy comes from people being on leave or absent.)

The bank also developed a holistic Triple E framework to create a meaningful learning environment for their people and assist them to progress in their careers. Its components included education, experience and exposure.

- Education—integrated learning experiences including role plays, simulations, mobile and social learning and hackathons
- Experience—cross-country and cross-functional assignments, international mobility, participation in strategic task forces and short-term rotations
- Exposure—systematic networking with senior leaders as well as mentoring and coaching

Bank leaders want DBS to be a "university" of banking talent, a place where people could learn and grow while making a difference at work. These leaders worked hard creating the right talent programs. They asked, "What exposure are people missing? What jobs should they do? What are the next jobs they should have? What skills do they need?"

> "We focused on two aspects in developing the people agenda: One was to create an overarching work environment that made it simple for people to work. And for employee engagement, we accepted what people were telling us and tried to figure out what we needed to focus on."
> —Piyush

To encourage employee engagement and nurture talent from within, the bank adopted a new internal mobility policy: "2+2" and "3+3":

- 2+2—AVPs and below can apply for another role within the bank after two years and, if accepted, their supervisors have to release them within two months.
- 3+3—VPs and above can apply for another role within the bank after three years and, if accepted, be released from their current position within three months.

By 2014, employees underwent an average of 45.6 hours of training, about a quarter of DBS's positions were filled by internal transfers and over 50% of new hires came from employees' referrals.

Employees have a good understanding of DBS's strategy and are motivated by the company's mission and vision. This is shown by the Gallup's Q12 Engagement survey which has improved from 4.0 in 2010 to 4.36 in 2014 (5.0 being the maximum), placing DBS at the 95th percentile of all companies surveyed by Gallup globally. Consequently, the retention rate has improved every year. Increasingly more people are choosing to grow their careers with DBS, making this bank one of the best-in-class compared to its industry peers. The heavy investment in its people, real estate, infrastructure and technology meant the bank was on the way to Building Excellence.

Excellence in Execution Challenges

Build Excellence

As a leader, how do you:

- Know what needs to be communicated continually?
- Identify the right measures to track performance?
- Create a culture of excellence that supports your new strategy?
- Identify areas you need to excel at to execute the strategy?
- Eliminate non-value-added work?
- Innovate the way you work to align with the strategy?

Terms & Tools: Culture of Excellence (CoEx), Abandon Yesterday, Strategy Scorecard, Strategy Map, Balance Scorecard, Vital Few, Big Data, Synergize, Process Owners, "To-stop" List

Materials featured in this book are available at www.implementation-hub.com/tools_tips_techniques/excellence-in-execution

—— *Chapter Eleven* ——

Build Excellence

 Video Quiz: What do 84% of business leaders believe is critical to business success?

*Y*our execution is gaining traction. You have Created Awareness and people understand why the organization must transform. They have become engaged, know the right actions to take and have acquired the necessary skills. You are on the path to achieving Excellence in Execution.

When you Build Excellence, you leverage these achievements and are providing updates on the progress against the strategy objectives, encouraging people to take the right actions, discussing lessons learned, sharing best practices and examining how the strategy affects the way people work. People are seeing how their actions contribute to the organization-wide strategy.

In Build Excellence, you also address the change in the measures used, introduce new policies, adopt new work methods and, if required, shift the culture.

Your culture drives the way you make the execution your own.

It's important to note that, in making the execution your own, you may have taken on a different approach. For example, it's not uncommon in some organizations to identify the measures for the strategy at the start of Create Awareness. Also, the Second Wave of Communication—constantly communicating progress against the strategic objectives—is prevalent in the Build Excellence phase. Many organizations falter at this point as they lack the discipline and the right culture.

Culture that Reflects Excellence for Execution

Culture in an organization can be defined as the way you do everything. Your culture determines how you run a meeting, how you communicate, how you launch a new product, what type of people you attract and retain, and how people dress and behave. That includes acceptable dress code and times they arrive at and leave work. As culture affects people's attitudes and actions, it's also what differentiates you from your competitors. It's what makes HP different from Dell, JP Morgan different from Citigroup and Southwest Airlines different from Singapore Airlines.

Culture defines an organization's personality and how it achieves Excellence in Execution.

A strong organizational culture is one of the most sustainable competitive advantages an organization can have because it is difficult to replicate.

When Booze & Co (now Strategy&) interviewed 2,200 leaders, 84% of the interviewees said culture is critical to business success.[78] *This is the answer to the video quiz.* More than half also said that culture is not well managed; it is mismanaged and undervalued.

---

78 http://www.strategyand.pwc.com/global/home/what-we-think/reports-white-papers/article-display/cultures-role-organizational-change

In addition, AT Kearney reported that 62% of business executives said crafting and executing strategy has become more complicated over the past decade and that 80% of executives globally considered agility as important as or more important than strategy.[79]

Strategy Cadence and Culture

When your Strategy Cadence is too fast for your organization's culture, you can end up with *overpromise and under deliver,* risking failure for the whole execution. In contrast, if the Strategy Cadence is too slow for your culture, then momentum is lost, Mavericks become disheartened and the execution can fail. Leaders are responsible for determining the right Strategy Cadence for the organization's culture.

> *Powerful Execution Tip*: Of the eight directions on the Implementation Compass, culture is the hardest to execute with excellence. This is because culture permeates everything in an organization.

 ### The Impact of Culture in Your Organization

When preparing to roll out your strategy, assess how your culture affects its execution by asking these questions:

1. How do we define our organizational culture?
2. What have we executed in the past successfully?
3. How did our culture contribute to the success?
4. What has failed in the past and why?
5. How did our culture contribute to the failure?
6. What is unique in the way we work that makes us successful?
7. What are the stories told about our organization?
8. Who are the heroes and what stories are told about them?
9. How do our people perceive our culture?
10. What adjectives describe our culture?

---

79 https://www.atkearney.com/strategy/futureproof-strategy/the-state-of-strategy-today

By reviewing the answers to these questions, leaders can start to define their own culture and answer in detail this concluding question:

11. *How will the culture contribute to achieving Excellence in Execution?*

Each organization executes its strategy differently based on its own way of doing things. Consider that Singapore Airlines' culture calls for building consensus through meetings and discussing key decisions among the leaders. Apple Computer has no committees while Google's culture thrives in a fact-driven environment.

In another example, Oracle acquired more than 100 companies in five years. Its leaders don't talk of mergers and acquisitions (M&A) but only acquisitions. Whether it's Sun Microsystems or PeopleSoft or SelectMinds, Oracle has had to absorb dozens of other organizations into its culture. Oracle's culture is said to be autocratic, but then how can an organization successfully acquire so many others and also entertain everyone's opinions in the process?

In these examples, the leaders understand the impact of culture on execution and they leverage it to create positive results.

Note that culture doesn't always have a positive impact on how people in an organization behave. In Enron's competitive atmosphere, for example, to stop other traders from sabotaging them, people had to lock their computer screens when they went to the restroom. Otherwise, these other traders would change their positions on trades to make them look bad. No one helped each other.

**"You must create a culture of trust and
commitment that inspires people to execute
the strategy, not to the letter but to the spirit."
—W. Chan Kim and Renee Mauborgne, *Blue Ocean Strategy***

Powerful Execution Tip: When you drive your team to take the right actions, you initiate building a Culture of Excellence—CoEx.

The goal of creating a Culture of Excellence—CoEx—eludes many organizations mainly because achieving it takes considerable time, effort and discipline.

> **"Companies that are great at both strategy and execution tap the power of the ingrained thinking and behavior that already exists below the surface, using culture, not structure, to drive change."**
> **—Paul Leinwand, Cesare Mainardi, Art Kleiner**

 ## Creating a Culture of Excellence (CoEx)

Five key building blocks for creating a CoEx are:

1. Pay attention to the details.
2. Hold people accountable.
3. Reinforce excellence and don't accept poor performance.
4. Be transparent.
5. Never settle.

Each of these building blocks is explained while leveraging Singapore Airlines (SIA) as an example for each one. Thank you to Marvin Tan, Senior Vice President Product & Services, for taking the time to share how SIA builds a CoEx.

These five building blocks are specific to when you are achieving Excellence in Execution. In isolation, they will not achieve CoEx.

1. Pay Attention to the Details

This means taking care of the small stuff, but it doesn't mean micro managing your people. They need to be *empowered* to take the right actions and know the parameters of the empowerment. As a leader, you need to assess the details to make sure you're moving in the right direction on the implementation journey and stopping small issues from becoming big problems. Just like any journey, you constantly check where you are against your destination and handle challenges as they occur.

The "broken windows" theory[80] developed by the late James Q. Wilson emphasizes beautifully why paying attention to detail is important. This theory states that "Signs of disorder will lead to more disorder. A building with a broken window that has been left unrepaired will give the appearance that no one cares and no one is in charge. This will lead to vandals breaking the rest of the windows and adding graffiti because in their minds nobody cares." The criminal offenses will then become more severe. In execution, you need to pay attention to the details, to convey its importance and to stop people from taking the wrong actions.

SIA demonstrates this in how it trains new cabin crews. Through their 15½ weeks of training (longer than any other airline), trainees are taught specifically how to serve passengers and how to dress. They are even taught how to place the glass in front of the passenger with the SIA logo facing them (otherwise, what's the point of having the logo on the glass!). In 2013, the grooming standards for the crew were refreshed to maintain the right first impression. Female crew members are taught how to tie their hair and put on their makeup. Details even came down to the length of eyelash enhancements female crew members could wear.

SIA's high standards also extend to its service partners. In the 1980s, SIA realized there was no point offering exceptional service in the air if the service on the ground didn't match it, so its leaders worked with Changi Airport in Singapore to create a positive customer experience. Changi Airport, which has been voted in many different surveys as the best airport in the world, is extremely careful about managing details. When an aircraft touches down and stops at the gate, the first piece of luggage is on the conveyer belt within 12 minutes and the last within 40 minutes. Not only is this important for arriving passengers, but it reflects a comprehensive system that facilitates passenger connections. Two examples are the Immigration area clears a passenger every eight seconds and taxi drivers wait at the back of their taxis to assist their passengers with their luggage.

---

80   http://study.com/academy/lesson/broken-windows-theory-definition-lesson.html

Both SIA and Changi Airport have built a CoEx by paying attention to the detail.

2. Hold People Accountable

Chapter Seven introduced the importance of accountability in organizations that achieve Excellence in Execution. It's mentioned again here because it's an indispensable building block.

Accountability in Execution in Excellence between leaders and employees includes these steps:

- **Know the organization's core values.**—The values act as guiding principles of what is important and acceptable.
- **Clarify expectations.**—People need to know how they are expected to perform and what they're expected to deliver based on values *before* they can be held accountable. For example, does accountability mean attending meetings on time and/or submitting reports on time and/or checking that the right actions have been taken?
- **Adopt measures.**—Putting in place the right measures allows you to track performance, show what's important and hold people accountable.
- **Assign one person.**—You can't have more than one person responsible because that eradicates the accountability.
- **Conduct reviews.**—People need to know they'll be asked how they did against the defined actions on a regular basis.
- **Link actions to consequences.**—People have to be recognized in a positive way when they take the right actions. There also needs to be negative consequences for inertia or the wrong actions, and the consequences have to align with the values.

In SIA, the employees are held accountable for demonstrating the airlines' core values: Pursuit of Excellence, Safety, Customer First, Concern for Staff, Integrity and Teamwork. Due diligence is conducted on new hires to ensure they have integrity. Cabin crews are held responsible for owning customers concerns onboard a flight. Onboard issues are captured in a "voyage report" and tracked for review and follow up internally.

3. Reinforce Excellence and Don't Accept Poor Performance

People often struggle to understand which actions are important in the implementation journey, especially at the start. Leaders need to frame the CoEx by setting the right standards and encouraging people to strive to reach them.

Reinforcing excellence clarifies what is important, just as not accepting poor performance clarifies what is not acceptable. This prevents poor performance and encourages employees to strive for excellence.

In SIA, leaders strongly communicate the airline's positioning statement "Great way to fly" and the "most awarded airline" internally. In their service development, they aim to set new industry standards and "wow" their customers. Cabin crews have OBA (onboard assessments) for grooming, uniform turnout, interaction with passengers, product knowledge, safety and security, team spirit and job skills. Their annual appraisal also has a 10% allocation for passenger feedback with the rest being made up of OBA (60%), Discipline (15%), Attendance Record (10%) and Ward Leader Assessment (5%). Using these criteria, crew members are assessed on their performance in a clear, structured manner.

4. Be Transparent

Leaders at times limit what they share or even camouflage information. When employees discover this, it can form doubts in their confidence and even derail developing CoEx. It's best when leaders lead by example and are transparent so their people are also transparent.

In its 2004 research, the Economist Intelligence Unit reported that top performing organizations are distinguished by having greater transparency than those not at the top.[81] These organizations also make better use of performance data and measurement mechanisms, and they have built stronger communication channels between leaders and employees.

---

81   http://graphics.eiu.com/files/ad_pdfs/celeran_eiu_wp.pdf

SIA demonstrates transparency in how it assesses its people and encourages its crew to submit reports on onboard issues and incidents. A senior crew member conducts preflight briefings for the cabin crew. The briefings cover the order of service, special needs passengers, safety standards and emergency procedures. They also provide a forum to asking questions.

5. Never Settle

"Today's excellence is tomorrow's standard" has been one of my statements for decades. As soon as you sit back on your laurels, your competitors will punish you. In quality circles, this constant effort to improve is referred to as "continuous improvement" or "kaizan." SIA has made a profit every year over the last 29 years—through wars, recessions and high oil prices. The mantra "never settle" is embedded in Singapore Airlines' DNA. Its people challenge themselves to improve as they implement the next strategic initiative. The airline's milestones have included:

- In the 1950s, SIA was the youngest fleet.
- In the 1960s and '70s, it was service in the air.
- In the 1980s and '90s, it was OSG—Outstanding Service on the Ground.
- In the mid-1990s, it was technology in the air.
- In the mid-2000s, it was TCS—Transforming Customer Service—and SOAR—Service Above All the Rest.

A recent example is SIA's announcement to relaunch the longest flight in the world. It will go from Singapore to New York starting in 2018 and flying a variant of the lighter and more fuel-efficient A350 aircraft. The airline had previously operated the route with the A340-500 aircraft but the economics proved challenging. Despite this experience, Singapore Airlines recognized the demand for such a service and seized on the opportunity with advanced technology.

Because of its culture, SIA's initiatives ensure employees know they must take the right actions in the right way. Its leaders lead by example as they show that, without a CoEx in place, it's difficult (if not impossible) to achieve Excellence in Execution.

> *Powerful Execution Tip*: Mistakes will be made in execution. Dealing with them in the right way contributes to your culture and encourages people to learn from them and keep moving forward.

Make It Your Own and Amazon Entering India

Although you can examine principles and adopt tools that work in other organizations, the approach you adopt must fit your organization's unique culture. Working out how to make it your own is a constant challenge throughout the journey. When you attain it, you're well on the way to achieving Excellence in Execution.

> *Powerful Execution Tip*: Every organization's culture is different. Just as your unique culture drives the implementation journey, every execution must be unique.

The entry of Amazon.com (Amazon) into India provides a good example of making the execution your own. In the United States, most people have access to the internet, a home address and an option of delivery organizations. That's not true in India.

Amazon entered the Indian market in 2013 by offering access to products that millions of people have never been able to buy or afford before—a shop window for making dreams come true. It predicts that, in just a few years, India will be second only to the U.S. market in its size. Combined, the countries of China, India and U.S. will account for nearly 50% of the global smartphone market by 2017, and Goldman Sachs claims that the Indian e-commerce market will be worth over $300 billion by 2030, a 15-fold increase.[82] Amazon adds a staggering 40,000 products a day as well as selling 30 million

---

82 http://articles.economictimes.indiatimes.com/2015-05-07/news/61902484_1_flipkart-and-snapdeal-goldman-sachs-indian-ecommerce

products across hundreds of categories, with more than one million products in stock.

To succeed in India, though, Amazon has to make the execution its own. Its leaders have demonstrated their commitment to the process, investing more than US$5 billion. Amazon is expanding its network of warehouses and data centers while strengthening its marketplace platform ecosystem for its service. Its unique challenges require Amazon to have a different execution plan in India than in other countries.

"We're adapting to the local model."
—Jeff Bezos, CEO Amazon

The three elements of its plan include:

1. Internet access
2. Delivery and payment system
3. The competition

1. Internet Access
In India, around one third of the population can currently access the internet either from a computer or on a smartphone. But the telecommunications industry is growing; by 2017 it's expected that 33% of the Indian population will use smartphones. To overcome the limited internet access, Amazon has placed computers in stores where owners assist people who are unfamiliar with the internet. To reach potential customers through advertising, Amazon uses billboards and lucky draws.

2. Delivery and Payment System
Reaching customers with their orders and receiving payment are distinct execution challenges in India. To overcome them, Amazon had to redesign its business model. Some addresses in India are hard to find. So instead of delivering its distinctive brown boxes to customers' homes, they may be sent to a designated

neighborhood store—not by FedEx or UPS but by an army of Amazon motorbike delivery people.

Because some people in India don't own credit cards the owners of these designated stores collect COD (cash on delivery) on behalf of Amazon. They inform customers when their package arrives and receive a small commission for their efforts. They like the arrangement because as well as the commission, it drives business to their shops where people purchase other items.

3. The Competition

Amazon doesn't have a monopoly on the internet shopping market. It has to compete with local firms such as Flipkart (about 37% market share) and Snapdeal (about 14%) and a newer entrant, Tata, which is starting to see success. Six months after entering the market in India, Amazon had attracted half the amount of traffic Flipkart had built up in six years. According to comScore, within three years of entering the market, Amazon became the most visited e-commerce site in India and has about 24% market share.[83] Its number of visits overtook Snapdeal in 2016.

> "The biggest surprise is how fast our size in India has grown. I never guessed we would become this size in just over two years."
> —Diego Placentini, Senior VP for International Business, Amazon

By comparison, Amazon's revenue in the third quarter of 2015 in the U.S. was 81% greater than its combined revenues from the rest of the world. However, this is changing. CEO Jeff Bezos estimates that, in record time in India, Amazon will surpass US$1 billion in retail sales. This represents a better foray than its entry into China in 2004. There, Amazon has struggled especially against Alibaba and, in 2016, has less than 2% market share in China.

Flipkart (whose founders both worked at Amazon before leaving in 2007 to create their own start-ups) is going head to head with Amazon to win business,

83   http://www.ibtimes.co.in/amazon-overtakes-snapdeal-become-no-2-e-tailer-676585

but each has its own execution style. A recent survey in 2016 identified Amazon as India's most trusted online shopping brand.[84]

Two organizations can be heading in the same direction with similar strategies. However, their execution will always be different because of their cultures and the language they use.

The Language Effect

Part of making culture your own is the language used in your organization. A classic example is Disney calling its engineers "imagineers" and, in its theme parks, the terms Guests, Cast Members, VoluntEARS and the Show are used.

Recognizing the importance of language, Singapore Public Service created an approach to ensure customers don't hear that dreaded excuse "It's not our department." Its leaders started an initiative called "No Wrong Door." That means any time someone calls a government department, the person answering will manage the call until he or she reaches the right department, even if it's from a completely different part of the government.

When you move from crafting the strategy to executing it, it's beneficial to use terms and language people relate to as the organization builds a CoEx. Take into account the preferred language of the new strategy and the impact you want it to have on your people.

See Figure 11.1 on the next page as an example.

Strategy Now Eats Culture for Dinner!

One of the late Peter Drucker's most famous quotes is "Culture eats strategy for breakfast." This is no longer always true and, in fact, it can more often be the other way around. Because of the accelerated pace of change in business today, strategy tends to eat culture.

The landscape has altered dramatically since Drucker's day. Today, with businesses moving faster than at any time in history, pace has dramatically reshaped the relationship among the elements of strategy, culture and execution.

---

84 http://economictimes.indiatimes.com/articleshow/51258066.cms?utm_
source=contentofinterest&utm_medium=text&utm_campaign=cppst

Figure 11.1

Language when Crafting Strategy		Language of Excellence in Execution
Strategy creation	→	Execution
Analyze and planning	→	Implementation
Thinking	→	Doing
Initiate	→	Follow-through
Leadership	→	Whole organization
Goal setting	→	Goal achieving

In Drucker's era, a strategy for an organization could span for 10 years and assumed a decade of stability and growth. Today, most are working in a medium or fast Strategy Cadence (Cadence is their speed of implementation), which means the strategy has to change every three years or so. This fast pace of change also means the organizational culture is constantly in a state of flux and is more readily influenced by rapidly transforming strategic decisions.

In 2014, Constellation Research stated, "Since 2000, 52% of the companies in the Fortune 500 have either gone bankrupt, dropped out, been acquired or ceased to exist."[85] Former CEO John Chambers of Cisco claimed that 40% of companies will be gone in 10 years, adding that "Either we disrupt or we get disrupted." The BBC reported that Professor Richard Foster from Yale University said that by 2020, more than three-quarters of the S&P 500 will be made up of companies unknown in 2016.[86]

---

85 https://www.constellationr.com/content/research-report-inside-2015-boardroom-priorities-parts-1-2
86 http://www.bbc.co.U.K./news/business-16611040

The relationship affecting strategy, culture and execution is shifting. To accentuate this shift, the question to consider is, "Does strategy drive culture or does culture drive strategy?" Strategy is about crafting the organization's future; it can't be constrained by the culture. To support the strategy, the culture may need to be adjusted. When crafting strategy, leaders have to keep an open mind and avoid limitations the culture may place on the vision.

Culture does not drive strategy.
Rather, culture drives the way you execute.

People who argue that culture drives strategy say culture is extremely difficult to change, that it dominates more than strategy. This may have been true in the past, but it can no longer be a valid way to think about or conduct business due to the fast pace that business models are required to transform. When it's said businesses today must be "agile," this largely refers to the agility of the organization's culture in response to the rapidly changing strategic direction. See Figure 11.2.

Figure 11.2

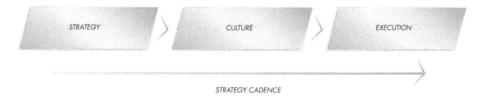

STRATEGY > CULTURE > EXECUTION

STRATEGY CADENCE

Keeping the culture nimble requires constantly adjusting it to support the execution of the strategy. The paradox is that organizations are built to be stable, yet they must keep transforming!

"Leadership is not about maintaining the status quo,
but maintaining the highest rate of change that the
organization and the people within it can stand."
—Sir John Harvey-Jones, English businessman

People adopt a new culture when it's clear the current strategy threatens the individual's future. Leaders must be able to demonstrate this. Here's an example.

Microsoft's CEO Satya Nadella announced to employees in 2014 that Microsoft Windows' monopoly was under attack and the organization needed to function more effectively.[87] Nadella's goal was to reduce the amount of time and energy needed to get things done in the engineering area. The cultural change required reduced the people involved in making decisions, thus making each individual more accountable. This shift has been changing Microsoft's culture.

At Microsoft, *strategy* now regularly eats *culture* for dinner. Organizations need an agile culture that embraces the accelerated pace of doing business and readily supports rapidly shifting strategies.

Abandon Yesterday (Not Hope!)

As life cycles of an organization's culture are becoming shorter, strategic inflection points (transition to a new strategic business model) are becoming more frequent. What worked yesterday no longer guarantees to add value to the business tomorrow.

Note that in 1985, 35% of stocks on the S&P were considered high risk (risk being based on the ability to achieve long-term stable earnings growth), 24% were average risk and 41% were low risk. By 2006, only 13% were low risk, 14% were average and a whopping 73% were high risk—and this was shortly before the Global Financial Crises of 2008! Also note that, in the 1950s, the average tenure of an organization listed in the S&P 500 was 61 years. Today, the average viable tenure of an organization was deemed 18 years. Consequently, leaders have to design and *execute* new strategies more frequently than ever before.

> *Powerful Execution Tip*: Achieving Excellence in Execution enables you to manage the accelerated pace of business and to beat your competitors. To do this, be prepared to release the past and seize the future.

---

87   http://www.pcworld.com/article/2452820/nadella-on-microsofts-culture-change-nothing-is-off-the-table.html

Business Model Disruption (BMD)

A new strategy requires changes to the current operating model—sometimes minor adjustments and at other times radical transformation. Sometimes the disruption is externally forced while other times it's internally driven.

> *Powerful Execution Tip*: To disrupt your organization, create an internal skunk team (team that adopts a radical approach) with the mandate to identify what would put the organization out of business!

Examples of BMD

Netflix is an excellent example of BMD by not revealing its viewership (as other do). The organization buys a whole program season without a pilot (as others request) and releases full seasons in one go. Netflix streams them without ads because people pay a subscription rate to receive them. In 2015, the company's stock rose 134%, which was the best performance of any Fortune 500 organization.

McDonald's has constantly leveraged BMD and internally driven initiatives that people said could not be done. In the mid-1970s, for example, it adopted the fast-food drive-through experience. More recently, it started a delivery service and then "Create Your Taste," allowing customers to create their own meal components.

Amazon is also leveraging BMD with its launch into brick-and-mortar stores. In addition, Encyclopedia Britannica and Toys R Us are making changes, discussed in detail here.

Encyclopedia Britannica

Encyclopedia Britannica was founded in Edinburgh, Scotland, in the 18th century. The organization took three years to create its first edition of encyclopedias. Twice in the last 20 years, Encyclopedia Britannica has been externally forced to respond to BMD (Business Model Disruption) and has reinvented itself to survive.

In 1990, Britannica's business peaked with 2,000 sales people selling over 100,000 units and its revenue approximately $650 million. In 1991, people started owning their own PCs and using CD-ROMs. Aware of changes in consumer behavior, Britannica created and sold its first CD-ROM for US$1,200 in the early 1990s. Then Microsoft created Encarta encyclopedia, also as a CD-ROM, which was positioned as a loss leader to sell Windows software to families. (Microsoft approached Britannica on developing a multimedia version of Britannica for PCs in the 1980s. Britannica declined.)

In response to Microsoft's move, Britannica produced Britannica Online in 1994. By1996, only 3,000 hard-copy encyclopedias were sold and its door-to-door sales force was dismantled. The CD-ROM price dropped from US$1,200 to $200 within 12 months. With falling sales, the organization was sold in 1996 for only $135 million and continued to sell its online version.

Then in 2001, Wikipedia arrived on the scene, introducing another external disruption. Once again, Britannica was forced to redesign its model to survive. It did not choose to compete directly with Wikipedia in the online market. Instead, it competed to provide a high level of editorial quality through Britannica Online. Scholars around the world were engaged to review, revise and refresh its content. Parents preferred to pay for reliable, trustworthy knowledge for their children developed by scholars than direct to them to an encyclopedia that was considered not as reliable.

Today, 500,000 households subscribe to Britannica Online, with its digital edition being updated every 20 minutes. Over the past five years, it has seen 17% compound annual growth in its digital education services business and a 95% renewal rate.

Toys R Us

In another example, Toys R Us also identified the internet as a BMD in the 1990s. But it failed to execute its new strategy, which resulted in a decline in its reputation and its cash flow returns for almost 15 years straight. Once the leading retailer of toys, Toys R Us has dramatically fallen behind its competitors.

When Toys R Us leaders realized the internet would be a dominant force in retail, it logically created www.toysrus.com to have an online presence. At the time, it had a strong following and brand—a perfect mix for going online. It also already had warehouses stocked with inventory and relationships with multiple suppliers. The online business seemed like a natural extension to its current business, but Toys R Us failed to execute its strategy. Here's why.

Toys R Us was used to shipping large quantities of products to single stores for restocking. It was not set up to ship single products to multiple addresses. In the 1999 holiday season, the number of orders overwhelmed the organization, and it failed to deliver children's toys on time for Christmas. The resulting damage proved devastating to the brand. Customers resolved to abandon not only the online shopping but its physical stores, too.

Ask These Questions

To prepare your organization to address BMD (Business Model Disruption), consider these questions:

1. Who will be your customers in the future?
2. What will they expect?
3. What disruptive technologies might open up new opportunities?
4. Who will be your competition tomorrow?
5. Where will you need to invest?
6. What will success look like from your investment?

Leaders are forced to respond to BMD more often than ever before. That means they have to execute more frequently. This has changed the relationship affecting strategy, culture and execution, and it's why organizations must maintain a culture that's agile and open to transformation. It underscores that culture is driven by strategy.

The goal of execution is to deliver on the strategy promises. When leaders understand the relationship affecting strategy, culture and execution, they can achieve this. But when they don't, they can fail to deliver.

Strategy Scorecard

Leaders require a Strategy Scorecard to track the execution and manage the business.

If you don't have the right measures in place to track your progress, you won't know where you are along your implementation journey and which direction to head. Without the right measures in place:

- People become confused if they're told one thing but measured against something else. When this occurs, they will continue to take actions based on achieving the old measures, not the new ones.
- You can't accurately show progress made from the baseline data to the targets.
- You don't know how your execution is performing and therefore can't take corrective action.

Organizations that have achieved Excellence in Execution are distinguished by having an effective Strategy Scorecard. Once they complete the strategy, leaders translate it into objectives. Then every objective has at least one measure and, from there, the measures drive the actions. Taking this approach and discipline to measurement serves to:

- Enhance leaders' understanding of the strategy across different business lines through the discussions generated
- Provide greater clarity about the strategy—what's important and what isn't
- Allow leaders to speak with greater consistency in their message by providing the strategy story
- Demonstrate both the importance and commitment to the new strategy

---

Measures are the means for managing the execution and the business. Without specific measures, leaders typically rationalize any outcome as they expected.

Powerful Execution Tip: When you adopt a new strategy, review and change current measures as required to avoid measuring yesterday's obsolete strategy.

Bridges uses the following model (see Figure 11.3) with its clients to assist them in transitioning from Vision to Performance.

The vision is the future state of the group. The mission is the core purpose. The values are the guiding principles. The strategy is the detailed plan on how you differentiate yourself from your competitors and how you will achieve the vision. Strategy objectives are identified to further translate the strategy. Every strategy objective has at least one measure. Every measure has an identified baseline and target attached to at least one action on how

Figure 11.3

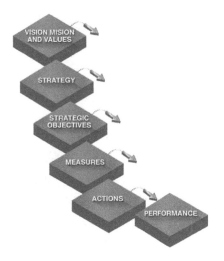

the organization will achieve the targets. Individuals are then held accountable for the actions they own. These actions are constantly reviewed to ensure the organization is on the right path toward the vision and delivering expected performance.

A Strategy Scorecard is an exceptional tool for measuring and managing strategy. Like many other business tools, using it must become part of the DNA of the organization.

Creating a Strategy Scorecard is not easy. The Bridges approach requires spending two days off-site with the leaders responsible. On the first day, participants refine their strategy map. Bridges interviews leaders in advance and presents the first draft of the strategy map at the off-site. Leaders also discuss the cause-and-effect relationships affecting the objectives on the map.

Then at a later time, they take two days to create the Scorecard and define actions. At a final half-day meeting, they review information and then initiate adopting the map and the Scorecard across the business.

When the Strategy Scorecard is adopted correctly, it ensures the organization can:

- View the progress of the execution at all times
- Make the necessary adjustments along the way
- Know that the right actions are being taken
- Know if the right outcomes are being delivered
- Communicate facts, figures and success stories about the execution's progress
- Reward and recognize people for their correct performances

"Measurement is the first step that leads to control and eventually to improvement. If you can't measure something, you can't understand it. If you can't understand it, you can't control it. If you can't control it, you can't improve it."
—H. James Harrington, performance improvement expert

Powerful Execution Tip: Some people confuse goals as measures and vice versa. Use losing weight as a simple analogy. The goal is to be slim and the measure is how much weight is lost each week.

The right measures drive the right actions. After selecting a measure for each strategic objective and identifying a team's performance, leaders have a baseline to work with. They then set a target over a period of time and spell out the action(s) required to achieve the target. See Figure 11.4 for an illustration of this.

Figure 11.4

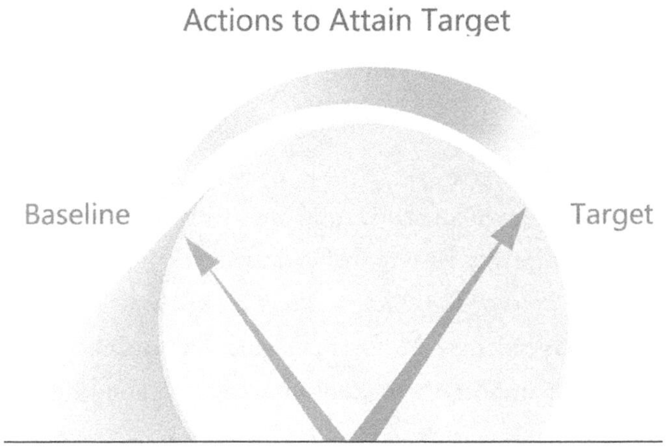

Actions to Attain Target

Baseline   Target

Customer Annoyance

A personal favorite measure I introduce as a reality check for the execution is *customer annoyance*. That's when we seek to know how annoyed customers are. It doesn't mean counting the number of customer complaints each month; complaints are reactive. Rather, it requires sales people to ask their customers this question: *What have we done to annoy you?* Their answers establish an understanding of where the organization is currently performing and indicates when customers start to observe improvements from the strategy.

To identify the right measures, don't ask, "What should we measure?" Instead, ask, "What are the specific strategic objectives?" and "How will we know if we are successful?"

Powerful Execution Tip: The right metrics drive the execution; the wrong ones can derail it, which is why it's essential to have an effective Strategy Scorecard.

When crafting the Strategy Scorecard, leaders also commonly ask, "How many measures should a scorecard have?" *There is no right number*. Because you need to have a measure for every strategy objective, the number will depend on the complexity of your strategy and business. Create, however, only the *vital few*—those measures needed to manage the business and ensure you track all your strategy objectives.

The Vital Few

Before creating a Strategy Scorecard, most measures seem as if they'd be good to have. Yet your objective isn't to be inclusive; it's just the opposite. *Select only the measures that track the strategy execution against the strategy objectives.* Some measures discussed may be for managing the business and operational performance. They're important to know but should not be included in the Strategy Scorecard.

Selecting the right measures means identifying the *vital few* rather than the *trivial many*.

Powerful Execution Tip: Have the discipline to refrain from including more measures than you need.

The Vital Few Guiding Questions

Ask these four questions for each measure selected:

1. Does the strategy objective have a measure?
2. Will the measure you're selecting assist you at a leadership level to measure and manage the business?
3. Is the measure essential for reviewing the execution or is it a "nice to know"?
4. Is it relatively easy to gather the required data (e.g., leveraging analytics)?

Once the right measures are in place, they guide you in managing the business toward your goal of achieving Excellence in Execution. In some organizations, decisions made at meetings are swayed by opinions and stories without having supporting facts and numbers. The Strategy Scorecard provides the required data. At Google, for example, people don't go by their "gut feelings." Rather, decisions are data driven so people have to present numbers to back up their views.

**"Every organization has only a handful of measures that are
truly critical to the successful execution of its strategy."
—Robert Simons, Charles M. Williams Professor of
Business Administration at Harvard Business School.**

Adopting Lead Indicators

It's one thing to *measure* the business and another to *manage* it. Effective measures drive decisions that guide the execution. A strategic objective requiring extra effort might need more than one measure to track performance. In that case, you might adopt *lead indicators* to drive actions that affect the objective.

As an example, consider the objective of losing weight. (See Figure 11.5.)

Figure 11.5

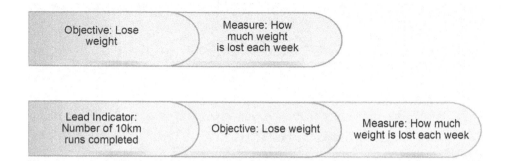

Measuring the number of 10 km runs not only adds focus to the objective of losing weight; it also drives the action of running 10 km as planned.

By regularly reviewing all the measures, you make small changes along the way that keep it on track. During your discussions, the changes may not appear overly significant, but the value of regularly reviewing your progress and making adjustments can't be overly stressed.

15 Best Practices for Using Measures to Manage the Business

After 20 years of developing and rolling out Strategy Scorecards across the world for various clients, I have identified these 15 best practices from organizations that achieve Excellence in Execution:

1. Translate your strategy into objectives.
2. Drive actions through measures.
3. Start leadership meetings with the Scorecard as item one on your agenda.
4. Address disconnects between what you say and what you measure.
5. Avoid using obsolete measures.
6. Adopt intangible and tangible measures.
7. Avoid feel-good measures.
8. Assess the complexity of the measures.
9. Recognize that statements are not measures.
10. Have confidence in numbers.

11. Discuss the Strategy Scorecard with board members.

12. Use a weathercaster's style—first the measure, then the reason behind it.

13. Link pay to performance.

14. Use measures to inspire.

15. Follow A2B formula.

Let's examine each of these best practices.

1. Translate Your Strategy into Objectives

Strategy objectives are the critical, must-achieve, make-or-break organizational performance outcomes. Use a short sentence (e.g., Build and leverage brand strength) that fits in the box for your strategy map. Set objectives to articulate what the strategy needs to accomplish. *Note: There is no right number of strategy objectives, just as there is no right number of measures.*

2. Drive Actions through Measures

Selecting the right measures and executing them is challenging because specific measures focus people on what to do. For example, as children, we adopted specific actions to gain pocket money; as adults, we adopt specific actions to earn bonuses. Be aware of the actions driven by the measures selected and constantly review the difference they make.

3. Start Leadership Meetings with the Scorecard as Item One on the Agenda

At the beginning of every leadership meeting, discuss relevant Scorecard measures and determine the progress made. This keeps the execution on the leaders' radar, allowing them to take action as required. It also emphasizes what's important and where to allocate time and resources.

Creating the strategy map and scorecard is relatively straightforward, but having the discipline to adopt them to manage the business can be challenging. Many organizations fail at it.

4. Address Disconnects between What You Say and What You Measure

Eliminate confusion around the execution of a new strategy as quickly as possible so people know what's expected of them.

Part of the confusion happens when leaders say one thing but measure something else. For example, in one organization, a strategy to improve customer satisfaction was set but no measure was attached to it. Instead, people were measured against the financial performance of the business, creating a disconnect. *In the long run, people take actions based on what leaders measure, not on what they say.* In this case, they took actions to increase sales and not to improve customer satisfaction.

These kind of disparages happen too frequently. Make sure your measures reinforce the strategy, the desired actions and the instructions you give.

5. Avoid Using Obsolete Measures

Many measures used in organizations today are the wrong ones because they haven't been recently reviewed and changed. Some leaders are guilty of using existing measures designed for an old strategy.

Any new strategy requires reviewing and adjusting its measures.

6. Adopt Intangible and Tangible Measures

Most organizations track a disproportionate number of tangible versus intangible measures. The investment firm Ocean Tomo estimated that, in 1975, more than 80% of the value noted in the S&P consisted of *tangible* assets. In 2010, approximately 80% of the S&P market value was attributed to *intangible* assets.[88] This indicates how the practice of tracking intangible assets has made a massive leap.

Historically, many measurement systems in organizations evolved from the agricultural period and have not been updated to reflect modern times. Baruch Lev of the Brookings Institution indicated, for example, that in 1982, 62% of the market value (measured by market capitalization) of organizations

---

88 http://www.oceantomo.com/ocean-tomo-300/

could be attributed to tangible assets and only 38% to intangibles.[89] Ten years later, the Brookings analysis of S&P 500 organizations showed that the relationship had been reversed: In 1992, it was 32% tangible to 68% intangible.

Interestingly, Apple is classified as a manufacturer by the U.S. government, yet it has 500 stores worldwide. Its revenue mostly comes from selling products, with all of its production outsourced. It also offers iCloud-related services. Apple rents out servers, which allows it to easily add or reduce capacity.

7. Avoid Feel-Good Measures

Classic examples of feel-good measures are the number of people attending trainings and the number of Facebook "Likes." Both measures are nice to report and easy to capture but aren't meaningful. Just because staff members have attended trainings doesn't mean they've adopted new competencies. And just because the organization has Facebook fans doesn't mean those fans are buying products. Effective measures would include an increase in the competency levels of people and the number of customers who purchased new products through Facebook promotions.

8. Assess the Complexity of the Measures

When identifying measures, what sounds like a good idea at the time can be hard to adopt after further scrutiny. After selecting a measure, ask, "What is the cost and what are the challenges in adopting this measure?"

For example, a fashion retailer wanted to measure conversion ratios—that is, the percentage of people who came into the store and did not buy versus those who bought something. Various complex schemes were proposed involving the use of radio frequency identification tags and various types of sensors. In the end, the organization decided on the simple concept of hiring students. The students sat outside of their stores and counted the number of people who went in and the number who came out carrying the store's shopping bags.

---

89 Blair, Margaret. (1995) *Ownership and Control: Rethinking corporate governance for the twenty-first century.* Washington, DC: The Brookings Institution, Chapter 6.

When considering which measures to adopt, err on the side of caution and choose uncomplicated ones.

9. Recognize that Statements Are Not Measures

In reviewing its yearly planning methodology, leaders of a global pharmaceutical organization identified problems using cut-and-dried statements as measures. For example, they'd say, "We will sell our new product to doctors." Either this has been achieved or it hasn't, but making this statement doesn't help measure performance over one year and make improvements for the next.

Compare this to saying you plan to run a marathon. The cut-and-dried measure is whether you do it or not. You don't know beforehand how prepared you are until you track the number of runs you do and over what distance. Other measures include how many kilometers you run each week to gain endurance and how many times you work out to gain strength. These indicate your progress toward being ready to run a marathon.

**A measure is expressed as an absolute
number or a percentage, not a statement.**

---

10. Have Confidence in Numbers

To be meaningful, you must have 100% confidence in the numbers reported. If you don't, this fact will undermine the execution. As technology improves and systems gather analytics without any human intervention, having this confidence becomes easier. Data gathered manually increases the opportunity for errors, takes time and can lead to a lack of confidence in the numbers.

11. Discuss the Strategy Scorecard with Board Members

Your board should never be surprised about what is happening in the organization. By regularly reviewing the Strategy Scorecard with board members, you make sure they are aware of the objectives and actions. Then they can offer meaningful assistance and guidance.

12. Use a Weathercaster's Style—First the Measure, then the Reason Behind It

Think about how the weather is reported on television. Weathercasters first report the temperature and then explain why that temperature will be accurate. In meetings, many leaders do the opposite; they explain the why and then report the measure. Reporting the numbers this way helps you:

- Have more powerful execution in your presentation
- Avoid disruptive questions that aren't relevant to the discussion
- Set up valuable discussions on what the numbers mean

13. Link Pay to Performance

When you tie pay and performance to strategy performance measures, it guides employees' actions, increases their engagement and improves productivity. By leveraging the measures to drive the right actions, the time and effort, employees become more inspired as their contribution is recognized and rewarded.

14. Use Measures to Inspire

What you measure is what people pay attention to. In Excellence in Execution, measures are leveraged to inspire people to contribute at a high level. Ensure they know what's expected based on what's measured. They must also know what will happen if they reach the goal *and* what will happen if they don't.

15. Follow A2B Formula

When identifying and reporting measures, adopt the format A (current) to B (target). For example: A $268,000,000 to B $350,000,000 in 12 months (A is the current revenue and B is the target revenue).

This straightforward best practice instills the discipline of showing where you currently are versus what you want to achieve. It also ensures you use numbers or percentages, not statements.

Big Data: Its Opportunities and Challenges

One area that drives BMD (Business Model Disruption) and affects business measures is big data.

Big data is the explosion of volume, variety, and velocity. It's revolutionizing the way business is conducted and supports you to achieve Excellence in Execution.

Big data allows leaders to measure and therefore manage more accurately than ever before. Insurance companies, for example, can track and identify the type of driver a person is by reviewing the data from a vehicle's computers. Based on that data, they can offer policies that fit the driver's habits.

With the amount of data generated between the Big Bang and the year 2000 being created every month now, it explains why leaders can get overwhelmed as they integrate key information into strategy execution. The volume of data for leaders to access is approximately five exabytes every day! (An exabyte is two to the 60th power of bytes. The prefix "exa" means one billion billion.) That means leaders are also receiving more varied information with greater velocity in real time (or almost real time) at unprecedented rates.

As an example, think back a few years to when a customer research survey took at least three months and cost around $50,000. Today, leaders can receive daily customer feedback from already established analytics at minimal cost.

"Without big data analytics, companies are blind and deaf, wandering out onto the web like deer on a freeway."
—Geoffrey Moore, management consultant and author

How do leaders use this overwhelming amount of data? Some organizations such as Google, Facebook and Amazon were created to leverage digital from the start. Older companies such as GE and Apple are transforming themselves—and fast.

In two more examples, Walmart collects more than three petabytes (equal to one thousand million million) of data *every hour* from its customers. Proctor & Gamble (P&G) has "Business Sphere and Decision Cockpits" on 50,000 employee computers. These "cockpits" track the consumer pulse of the brand.

Instead of reading spreadsheets and trying to decipher the information, P&G uses data visualization that helps users analyze exceptions and trends.

P&G's former CEO, Bob McDonald, staked out a mission to "digitize" the company's processes from end to end. In his Monday morning executive meetings, McDonald and his executive team would refer to Business Spheres from which they could see a global map of markets either growing or shrinking. They'd then examine the countries and categories ranging from laundry detergent and shampoo to potato chips and diapers. Business Spheres also assisted employees to see and understand a variety of data. Using Business Spheres today, P&G is able to compress the time needed for making decisions.

"Data modeling, simulation, and other digital tools are reshaping how we innovate."
—Bob McDonald, former CEO, Procter & Gamble

Powerful Execution Tip: Extract from the big data the small data (dataset that contains very specific attributes) that can have a big impact.

Socks and Underwear

The challenge becomes translating data into actionable information. Let's say you work in a department store in the men's section. Collecting data reveals that when male customers buy socks, they also buy underwear. How do you use this data?

When I ask this question in my workshops, participants tend to give these three kinds of responses:

- Some say they would place the two items together to encourage customers to buy both.
- Others say they would place the items at either end of the area to encourage customers to walk across the floor and possibly have more sales of other items.
- Yet others say they would offer bundle deals.

The key message is that there is no right answer. You'd have to execute the actions and track the performance and then compare the data to decide what to change.

Fuji Xerox states that researchers found that visuals in color increase people's willingness to read a piece of content by 80%.

Goal-setting: Good or Bad?

In recent years, our understanding about measuring and setting business goals has deepened, leading to recognizing the negative side of goal-setting. Here's an example of when having a goal can be bad. It comes from the New York City taxi industry.

Have you ever wondered why (aside from increased demand) it's hard to get a taxi in New York City when it rains? Even though taxi drivers have more customers when it rains, they work less. Why? The drivers reach their daily targets faster and go home earlier. A way to improve the number of taxis available would be for drivers to set *monthly* instead of *daily* goals.

This example comes from the stimulating article "Goals Gone Wild: The Systematic Side Effects of Over-Prescribing Goal Setting" by Lisa D. Ordonez, Maurice, E. Schweitzer, Adam D. Galinsky and Max H. Bazerman.[90] It stated that setting goals has been overdone and can even be harmful if it degrades employees.

Specifically, goal setting can narrow people's focus. The article quoted Staw and Boettger (1990) who documented the dangers of becoming too narrowly focused. In their experiment, they invited students to proofread a paragraph in a promotional brochure that contained both grammatical and deliberate content errors. The researchers found that individuals instructed to do their best were more likely to correct both grammatical and content errors than those who were given explicit goals to correct either grammar or content but not both.

---

90   http://hbswk.hbs.edu/item/6114.html

They also concluded:

- Failure to achieve goals may result in people becoming demotivated.
- Goals that are too challenging may cause people to take the wrong actions as they attempt to achieve them.
- Individuals with multiple goals are prone to concentrate on only one goal.
- Goal-setting can result in unethical behavior. In fact, departments or divisions may sabotage their own colleagues to achieve targets. This can also result in silo building.

It's possible to set goals that are too specific and end up narrowing people's views and even creating blind spots. A popular video on YouTube from Simons and Chabris (1999)[91] shows players passing a basketball. (If you have not seen it, you might watch it before reading on.)

Viewers are asked to count the number of times the players who are wearing white, pass the ball. In the video, a man in a gorilla suit walks across the screen, but most people miss that because they're focused on counting the basketball passes. That's a blind spot.

Identifying how to use goals—for example, how aggressive a goal should be—depends on how you make the execution your own. The right measures with the right goals inspire and move the execution along, whereas the wrong goals can do the opposite.

Synergizing Work to Strategy

Once you have the goals and measures in place, another essential building block for achieving Excellence in Execution requires examining how the strategy affects the way people work. Without synergizing current ways of working, the execution can quickly turn from a dream into a nightmare.

Powerful Execution Tip: Be sure to synergize the processes to the execution or people will struggle to embrace the strategy, causing failure.

Synergy can be defined as the interaction of two or more agents or forces—strategy and work—so the combined effect is greater than the sum of their individual effects.

For example, an insurance organization's goal was to differentiate itself by providing customers with a seamless and efficient experience. Its call center was one of its main touchpoints with customers. Unfortunately, the call center systems were horrendously slow. Employees were frustrated with its poor response time while on the phone with customers. "May I put you on hold while I gather the relevant information?" was commonly asked. Not only that, because calls took so long, the dropped call rate (numbers of calls kept waiting that are dropped before they are answered) was very high. This example shows a lack of synergy between the strategy and the processes set up to implement it.

In the past decade, immense progress in improving processes or transforming work has been made. Six Sigma and other quality initiatives have shown that process improvement is not about reducing defects or cycle time but about improving the bottom line. Just one project redesign can send a quarter of a million dollars straight to the bottom line through cost savings and increased revenue. That represents a phenomenal opportunity.

In Excellence in Execution, any and all assumptions, practices, policies, service level agreements, and more are open to being challenged and changed.

Powerful Execution Tip: No matter how much training you provide to your people, it will not show improvement if the way of working is not synergized with the strategy. Consider empowering your employees to make the necessary changes.

Questions Defining Areas to Excel

Among your team discuss these questions:

1.1 What do we need to be doing better than our competitors?

1.2 If we were a competitor, what would we do to knock our organization out of business?

1.3 What are our customers' expectations?

1.4 How do we anticipate the strategy affecting our current business model?

1.5 What will success look like when we have executed the new strategy?

1.6 Which key processes *hinder* the proposed new way of working?

1.7 Which key processes *support* the proposed new way of working?

To ensure synergy between the new strategy and the way people are working, ask these three critical questions across all business verticals:

1. What do we need to excel at to deliver the strategy?

2. How will we transform the way people are working?

3. How will we sustain the new level of performance?

Let's examine each of these questions.

1. What do we need to excel at to deliver the strategy?

It's during the HOW phase when leaders ask, "Where must we excel to execute the strategy?" Because an organization can't excel in every area of its business, it must identify which are most important based on the new strategy. It could be supply chain management (e.g., Walmart) or sorting and dispatching (e.g., FedEx) or design (e.g., Apple) or customer service (e.g., Singapore Airlines).

Answering this question represents a major strategic decision. The following questions further assist in the leadership team's discussion.

By answering these questions, leaders identify the critical changes in how people can work differently for the strategy to be executed. They can then make improvements and innovations.

2. How will we transform the way people work?

As many different methodologies are available, selecting the right approach isn't easy, so it's critical to ask the right questions such as these:

2.1   What are the goals of the strategy?

2.2   What are the objectives of the redesign?

2.3   What are the different methodologies available?

2.4   From previous process initiatives, what worked and what failed?

2.5   How will the culture impact the work redesign?

2.6   What are the capabilities, strengths and weaknesses of the organization?

2.7   What resources are available?

2.8   What budget is available?

2.9   Is the approach easy to adopt?

2.10   Is any external support required?

Discussing these questions fully can take time, but it's essential to do it before adopting the methodology. If you approve an approach and it fails, it can also derail the whole execution.

Bridges has worked with two organizations that adopted process redesign, but each used a different approach. One used a cross-functional redesign to improve processes over a six-month period. The leaders brought together top performers from the function areas of the process they were changing. Over three months, they mapped out the existing process and redesigned it. They then spent the next three months implementing the redesign and finally began harvesting the results.

The leaders in the other organizations focused on eliminating what they called "customer hours"—that is, they reduced the time it took customers to carry out a process. This redesign only took five days.

Neither approach is better than the other; it all depends on which methodology best synergizes the process with the strategy effectively and works best within the culture of the organization.

3. How will you sustain the new level of performance?

Once you have selected the methodology and initiated a redesign of how people work, focus on sustaining the new performance. Employee performance needs to be constantly reviewed and redesigned. To accomplish this, these three best practices from Excellence in Execution can be adopted:

3.1   Identify process owners

3.2   Track work performance

3.3   Align recognition

Here's what's involved for each.

3.1 Identify Process Owners

A discipline of Excellence in Execution requires assigning Process Owners to critical processes along the implementation journey. Critical processes are identified as those the organization must excel at to deliver the strategy.

Process Owners are leaders in the organization who have influence, respect and vested interests in a particular process. They are responsible for the performance of the processes, participating in reviews, championing necessary changes, tracking indicators and achieving targets. They also need to influence people and take corrective actions when required. This work only takes a couple of hours of the Process Owner's time each month.

3.2 Track Work Performance

The Process Owner's responsibility includes tracking performances. Although the frequency of the tracking varies for different processes, it typically occurs either weekly or monthly. Analytics and data visualization make it easy to observe variances. When issues occur, Process Owners use tools such as root cause analysis to identify the reason and initiate corrective action. At the same time, they continue to ensure actions taken bring about the desired outcomes.

3.3 Align Recognition

The Process Owner needs to recognize people when they contribute toward improving a process. Reinforcement can take on many forms, with one of the most powerful being praise. When an immediate boss says "thank you" with sincerity for a job well done, it gives people a sense of achieving something greater than what they could have done on their own. This makes it a major source of inspiration.

> *Powerful Execution Tip*: Money, the most expensive form of recognition, vanishes into people's purses or wallets. Instead, allow people to choose a tangible form of recognition such as a gift voucher.

Praise and tangible gifts such as a book or theatre tickets are more appreciated than money, which has diminishing returns as a motivator. For example, let's say the first time you demonstrate the right behavior, I give you $20. If I reward you with $20 every time you demonstrate the right action, then after 10 times, you have $200. Over time, any additional money has diminished in importance to you.

Have a "To-Stop" List

Because execution happens at ground level, people need to be empowered to take the right actions to improve their work. This includes being able to eliminate non-value adding work. To Build Excellence requires having "to-do" lists, but employees also need "to-stop" lists of actions that don't contribute to the new strategy.

Peter Drucker coined the term *purposeful abandonment*, which means if you want to grow your business, before you decide where and how, stop doing what's not working.

Powerful Execution Tip: Create the space for execution by empowering people to eliminate the non-value-adding work. Discard the outgrown, the obsolete and the unproductive.

When you provide the opportunity, empowerment and methodology for people to eliminate unnecessary tasks, they will stop doing non-value-adding work, improve what they *are* doing and rise to the occasion. Examples of non-value-adding work include sending out reports people don't need, redoing work, being on a conference call unnecessarily or checking work that's already been checked. Some (Mavericks) will be excited because leaders are finally providing the opportunity to change activities they believe impede progress.

In a large organization, up to 33% of people's work can be non-value-adding. When people eliminate non-value-adding work, they critically create space and free up resources to take the right actions.

As a leader, when you empower your people to create and follow a "to-stop list," they become more engaged and accomplish more in less time. For example, A.G. Lafley, in his turnaround of Procter & Gamble, established a portfolio of performance initiatives that gave priority to four core businesses. At the same time, he created a "not-to-do" list that included projects driven by technology rather than customer needs. What's more, he ensured every initiative—whatever its focus—included building mindsets and capabilities focused on customers and external partnerships.

In a dramatic example, when Steve Jobs returned to Apple as CEO in 1997, he made a decision that shocked everyone from the frontline to the board members. He announced he was devoting all of Apple's resources to only four products. That stopped more than 70% of the hardware and software product development going on, cancelling over 300 projects.

At the time, Apple was manufacturing dozens of different Macintosh desktops, laptops and servers in a range of variations. It was also designing and manufacturing lines of printers, digital cameras and other ancillary items.

Very few of these products were making a profit. Jobs' decision focused the organization on developing only two consumer desktops and portables and two professional desktops and portables. Jobs walked into a special board meeting where two dozen Apple products were displayed. Dramatically, he began taking them down one at a time until only four products were left. Those were the ones, he said, that would give Apple new life by differentiating it in the marketplace.

Two things followed: 1) more than 3,000 layoffs and 2) sinking profits. But this stroke-of-brilliance decision resulted in Apple's turnaround. In effect, it gave the engineers time and resources to design what *would* sell.

> **"We believe in saying no to thousands of projects so that we can really focus on the few that are truly important and meaningful to us."**
> **—Steve Jobs, founder, Apple Computers**

Powerful Execution Tip: Telling leaders and people to stop doing something is often harder than asking them to do something new. Take the time to identify and share what you want your people to stop doing, then allow them to address the few activities you need them to do.

 ### Eliminating or Exiting Current Business

Points for the leadership team to discuss:

- ✓ Should we exit from any current business because it's not part of the new strategy?
- ✓ What work from our existing way of doing things is no longer required?
- ✓ What work are we currently doing that is not adding value?
- ✓ If we stop sending out reports, what will be the repercussion?

When people adopt a "to-stop" list, they present the work they want to kill off to their immediate boss and/or the leader of the specific business, either in person or electronically. The request is reviewed and responded to within three working days. If it's refused, employees are given a reason such as not being aware of a strategic initiative. This step ensures any changes align with the strategy. Follow up must occur to see if these changes have produced the expected outcomes.

Check for Expected and Unexpected Outcomes

When you transform the way people work to synergize to the strategy, it won't always have the expected outcome. In fact, a new way of working can create the *wrong* actions, as this example from Jakarta, Indonesia, demonstrates.

Jakarta introduced the "3 in 1 Policy" to reduce traffic in its city center. Drivers had to travel with two passengers in the car or take longer routes around the perimeter of the city center, or they faced being fined. The expected outcome was to reduce the traffic in the city.

Instead of reducing traffic, however, the "3 in 1 Policy" created a whole new action. Leaving the freeway but before entering the city, drivers would pull over to pick up a passenger or two from a group of people waiting. Each passenger would be paid the equivalent of US$1.50 to accompany the driver through the city center. Clearly, the "3 in 1 Policy" wasn't driving the right actions. Instead of encouraging drivers to travel with friends into the city, it succeeded in spawning a new service.

In another example, anyone regularly traveling out of Tokyo at Narita International Airport is used to the long lines at Immigration. This wait, combined with the time to reach the airport from the center of Tokyo, prompted airlines to encourage passengers to plan for sufficient travel and boarding time. Yet while travelers line up to pass through immigration, the airport staff frequently asks people traveling on departing flights to identify themselves, and then they fast-track them through Immigration. This frustrates the passengers who arrived early and waited in line for a long time. It also results in some people arriving "later" rather than "earlier" for flights. This is not the outcome the airport wanted, and it added to the congestion. That's why it's important to ensure the transformation is driving the right actions and producing the expected outcome.

In Build Excellence, the strategy is truly embedded in the culture of the organization. The Strategy Scorecard keeps the organization moving forward in the right direction, ensuring people work on the right projects and actions. The challenge is to sustain progress, remain focused and frequently review while reinforcing people's efforts.

─────── *Chapter Twelve* ───────

Questions to Build HOW (Part Two)

n making the execution your own, you identify what needs to happen to Build Excellence while leveraging achievements to date and moving the organization along the implementation journey.

HOW Questions to Build Excellence

Your culture—defined as the way an organization does everything—drives the way you execute your strategy. Therefore, to provide sustainable competitive advantages, the execution and culture have to align.

Consider the impact of your organization's culture on the execution by asking these questions:

1. How is the organizational culture defined?
2. What has been successfully executed in the past?
3. How has the culture enabled success?
4. What has failed in the past and why?
5. How did the culture contribute to the failure?

189

6.   What is unique in the way the organization works?
7.   What are the stories told about the organization?
8.   Who are the heroes and what stories are told about them?
9.   How do people perceive the culture?
10. What adjectives describe the culture?

In reviewing the answers to these questions, leaders define their own culture and then answer this key question:

11. How will the culture contribute to achieving Excellence in Execution?

Building a Culture of Excellence (CoEx) takes time and discipline. To achieve that, ask these questions:

12. Is enough attention being paid to what's most important to the business? *People are busy and are not always working on what adds value.*
13. How are people held accountable for delivering to a higher standard? *This is a key component for achieving Excellence in Execution.*
14. Is excellence reinforced?
15. Is poor performance not accepted? *What are the repercussions for underperforming?*
16. Is the business transparent in sharing key information?
17. Is there a mindset of "never settle"?

The challenge is for organizations to customize the HOW so it becomes their own way of execution. Also ask:

18. Is the right language being used to express the focus on execution?

Today's accelerated pace of change has shifted the strategic landscape. Currently, strategy drives the execution that drives the culture. In your organization:

19. Does strategy drive culture or does culture drive strategy?

Today, many strategies have a short lifecycle that demands a fluid organizational culture. If the strategy changes and the culture lags, then this delay can dramatically impair the execution. Organizations are built to be stable and yet must also keep transforming. Moving forward requires letting go of what no longer adds value. To do this, ask:

20. What needs to be eliminated or exited to create the space for taking the right actions?

Moving forward also involves using the right language, which you can check by asking:

21. Are you using the language of execution?

To consider the disruption threat for your business, ask these questions:

22. Who will be your customers in the future?
23. What will they expect?
24. What disruptive technologies might open up new opportunities?
25. Who will be your competition tomorrow?
26. Where will you need to invest?
27. What will success look like from your investment?

To ensure you're progressing in the right direction along the implementation journey, you need signposts along the way, including a Strategy Scorecard and other measures. If you don't have them, you won't know where you are or which direction to head.

Among Excellence in Execution organizations, translating the strategy into objectives, identifying measures for each objective and using the measures to identify the right actions are powerful best practices.

To identify the right measures, don't ask "what should we measure?" Instead ask:

28. What are our specific strategic objectives?
29. How will we measure each of these objectives? *Ensure every objective has a measure.*

To find out if your Strategy Scorecard is effective, ask these questions:

30. Can leaders accurately check on the progress of the execution at any time?
31. Do the measures drive the required changes?
32. Are the measures driving the right actions?
33. Do the leaders know if the outcomes are being achieved?
34. Are facts and figures being shared and adopted as a means of updating people on the progress made?
35. Are people recognized for their improvements on the Scorecard?

It's important to only use the *essential* measures and not too many of them. Focus on the vital few by asking these questions:

36. Does each strategy objective have at least one measure? *This is critical.*
37. Is the measure essential for reviewing the execution or is it a "nice to know"?
38. Is it relatively easy to gather the required data?
39. Do the measures selected assist in measuring and managing the business?

Using a Strategy Scorecard needs to become part of the DNA of the organization. When you need to place more focus on a measure, adopt lead indicators.

To have confidence in the reported numbers and assist in setting goals, applying analytics such as Big Data can ensure this. As a leader, your role is to make sure the goals lead toward the right outcomes.

The Strategy Scorecard also assists in synergizing work throughout the organization. To accomplish this, focus on the processes your organization needs to excel at and how to sustain the new desired level of performance by asking:

40. Where does the organization need to excel to deliver the new strategy? *What is the key thrust of the new strategy?*
41. What does the organization need to do better than its competitors? *Where is your differentiation?*
42. If you were a competitor, what would you do to knock your organization out of business?
43. What are your customers' expectations?
44. How do leaders in your organization anticipate the strategy that will affect the current business model?
45. What will success look like when you have executed the new strategy?
46. Which key processes *hinder* the proposed new way of working?
47. Which key processes *support* the proposed new way of working?

To identify the best methodology for transformation, ask these questions:

48. What are the goals of the strategy? *It's always good to revisit this question.*
49. What are the objectives of the redesign?
50. What are the different methodologies available?
51. From previous process initiatives, what worked and what failed?
52. How will the culture affect the work redesign?
53. What are the capabilities, strengths and weaknesses of the organization?
54. What resources are available?
55. What budget is available?
56. Is the approach easy to adopt?
57. Is any external support required?

To sustain the new high level of performance, ask:

58. How will you keep the new level of performance going?

59. Who will be the Process Owner? *This needs to be a leader.*
60. How will leaders effectively track work performance? *Consider using data visualizations.*
61. How will leaders recognize and reward employees for their effort?

Part of achieving Excellence in Execution is telling people what to "stop" doing and empowering them with a license to walk away from non-value-adding work. When people eliminate work that doesn't contribute to the new strategy, they free up time and resources to do what does work. This overcomes employee complaints such as "I don't have the time." To do this, ask these questions:

62. Should you exit from any current business because it's not part of the new strategy?
63. What activities from the current way of doing things are no longer required?
64. What work is being done that is not adding value?
65. If you stop sending out reports, what will be the repercussions? Does anyone miss these reports?

This series of questions continues after the Follow Through chapter.

——— *Chapter Thirteen* ———

DBS Case Study to Build Excellence

*W*hen Piyush started the bank's transformation, an early focus was to "fix the plumbing" as he called it. Fixing core issues involved empowering people across the bank to (1) improve the processes, (2) improve the way they provided service and (3) invest in new technology. As the plumbing was fixed, it also started to change the culture of the bank—something he recognized had to happen from day one.

Specifically, Piyush wanted people to be empowered, which was defined as being expected to do the right thing, to make decisions and be accountable for them. The new performance appraisal supported the change in the culture by making people more accountable. Failures were accepted (with the caveat that it had undergone a proper thought process) to encourage people to try new things and participate. Policies and structures were redesigned to support the desired new way of working. Today, DBS Bank has an open culture in which employees are encouraged to reach out to the senior leaders.

In contrast, the old culture was highly formal. Not only were leaders called by their surnames but also by their titles when people addressed them. Piyush eliminated this practice immediately. On his third day, he told his secretary that if she didn't stop standing up and calling him "Mr. Gupta" when he walked into the office, she would be "fired" (in jest). This was one way he set about changing the culture.

> **"You cannot move if your culture does not support [it]."**
> **— Yan Hong, HR Director**

The goal was to evolve the bank's culture—something that can't be bought and needs to happen from within. Achieving this required restructuring the bank's customer service and internal processes. The platform called Asian Service involved empowering people to redesign how they were providing service to customers and then delivering the new processes across the bank. This initiative became the most compelling platform for evolving the culture. For example, it gave people the confidence to make decisions they could make rather than leaving decision-making to their bosses as they had previously done.

They referred to the service standards as RED (Respectful, Easy to deal with, Dependable). This simple acronym became the basis for transformative actions and therefore a change in culture. It was quickly followed by the creation of the Customer Experience Council and the Innovation Council—platforms to drive change in the customer experience and eventually a culture change, too. By leveraging the customer experience and innovation platforms, a tangible link was created to the need to think differently for the customer. This was something everyone could relate to.

> **"The messaging is important but just telling people what to be doesn't change them. So you need a platform, and the whole customer experience turned out to be the most compelling platform for driving the culture change."**
> **— Piyush**

The leaders also reinforced the bank's values PRIDE. It stands for Purpose-driven, Relationship-led, Innovative, Decisive and E! for Everything fun (see

Appendix A). If you had 10 goals and met all 10, you were average. To excel, you had to do more than the expected 10 *and* be in congruence with PRIDE. There was zero tolerance for those who achieved their targets but disrespected the PRIDE values.

Also improving the culture was introducing a "5@5" policy. Bank employees are notorious for long working hours, so the 5@5 initiative allowed staff members to go home at five o'clock on Friday afternoons—a breakthrough.

A move to new offices in Marina Bay Financial Centre Tower 3 in 2012 also positively affected the bank's culture. The move created an opportunity to leverage the new location's design in a way that built the culture and encouraged the right actions by controlling the environment. The bank heavily invested in making the new offices a fun place to work. For example, the offices with a beautiful view of the bay were designed as common meeting areas, not executives' offices. The building also has a gym, a dance floor and large breakout areas. Employees even have their own Starbucks.

The successful transformation of the culture has played a large part in DBS's success with customer experience and an innovative mindset being the soul of the company.

Right Measures

Piyush also recognized early on that the right measures had to be put in place.

He quickly realized that the Management Information System (MIS) was lacking. The bank did not know, for example, which branches or which segments were profitable. To measure that and more, he made the investment to develop the MIS.

**"We were flying blindly, so having a good
system of measures was extremely important."
—Piyush**

Some banks struggle with bringing risk data together with financial data because the systems are built differently. They can struggle with account planning, cross selling and customers analysis because of it. The new system that DBS built integrated the financial and risk data to overcome these challenges. The new systems ensured the efforts from different business lines were reflected in the MIS and not double counted. The efforts were then linked to the bonus pool, and the new MIS encouraged sharing across divisions. Within divisions, it allowed strong regional connectivity to the point that customers were complimenting the bank on the strength of its regional connectivity. The bank's MIS became recognized by people as a fair system and a powerful enabler.

Today, there are no arguments about the numbers produced. The internal MIS numbers are reported with confidence internally to the board and to the businesses and countries. Better yet, they allow employees to focus on constantly improving their performance.

While integrating the new MIS the leaders also addressed the Strategy Scorecard.

**"We made the Scorecard a living document,
which was very useful for us."
—Piyush**

Piyush and his team established a balanced scorecard approach to measure how successfully they were driving the execution of long-term strategy. The Scorecard, based on DBS's strategy, is used to set objectives, drive behaviors, measure performance and determine remuneration. In 2010, a Scorecard did not get completed until end of the first quarter, which made it hard to achieve targets. Changing the Scorecard itself as well as its completion date to before the end of the year signaled to leaders to take action before the end of the year.

The Scorecard was divided into two parts, each with equal weighting, hence the term balanced. The Top Half has traditional metrics balanced among shareholders, customers and employees. The Bottom Half has the long-term metrics indicating what the bank has to do every year as part of the development journey. It includes the nine strategic priorities. (See Figure 13.1 for the nine strategic points and DBS Bank's Scorecard in 2014.)

Figure 13.1

The Asian Bank of Choice for the New Asia

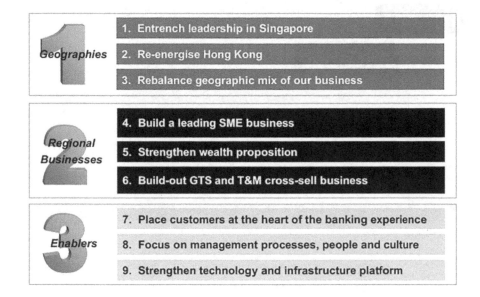

Geographies
1. Entrench leadership in Singapore
2. Re-energise Hong Kong
3. Rebalance geographic mix of our business

Regional Businesses
4. Build a leading SME business
5. Strengthen wealth proposition
6. Build-out GTS and T&M cross-sell business

Enablers
7. Place customers at the heart of the banking experience
8. Focus on management processes, people and culture
9. Strengthen technology and infrastructure platform

The DBS Scorecard is balanced in the following ways:

- Balanced between financial and non-financial performance indicators, with almost a third of the total weighting on control and compliance metrics
- Balanced across multiple stakeholders and not focused solely on shareholders
- Balanced between short-term and long-term outcomes

At the end of every year, every Management Committee (MC) member takes the Group Scorecard for the next year and identifies what each must deliver in his or her line of business. Then they share their individual Scorecards with the other MC Members for support and alignment. The Scorecard reflects what was achieved and measured, and it's highly transparent. Also used for setting budgets and bonuses, it's updated and discussed with the board for its approval. Once approved, it cascades throughout the organization, ensuring that the

Figure 13.2

Our 2014

Priorities

We are guided by a long-term perspective in line with the interests of our multiple stakeholders. Our balanced scorecard is used to set objectives, drive behaviours, measure performance and determine the remuneration of our people.

Our scorecard is based on our strategy, underpinned by the opportunities, risks and material matters that we have identified. The scorecard is divided into two parts of equal weighting. The first part of the scorecard comprises KPIs and strategic objectives set for the current year. The second part of the scorecard sets out the initiatives we intend to complete in the current year as part of our longer-term journey towards achieving our strategic objectives.

TRADITIONAL KPIs

SHAREHOLDERS	CUSTOMERS	EMPLOYEES
Achieve Sustainable Growth Shareholder metrics measure both financial outcomes achieved for the year as well as risk-related KPIs to ensure that the Group's income growth is balanced against the level of risk taken, including control and compliance. ❯ For more information, see page 28	**Position DBS as Bank of Choice** Customer metrics measure the Group's achievement in increasing customer satisfaction and depth of customer relationships. ❯ For more information, see page 35	**Position DBS as Employer of Choice** Employee metrics measure the progress made in being an employer of choice, including employee engagement and people development. ❯ For more information, see page 46

STRATEGIC PRIORITIES

GEOGRAPHIES	REGIONAL BUSINESSES	ENABLERS
• Entrench leadership in Singapore • Continue to expand Hong Kong franchise • Rebalance geographic mix of our business ❯ For more information, see page 44	• Build a leading small and medium enterprise (SME) banking business • Strengthen wealth proposition • Build out transaction banking and treasury customer business ❯ For more information, see page 36	• Place customers at the heart of the banking experience • Focus on management processes, people and culture • Strengthen technology and infrastructure platform
OTHER AREAS OF FOCUS	**REGULATORS**	**SOCIETY**
• Drive digital initiative including building infrastructure to digitise the bank • Cascade and embed our PRIDE! values • Affirm expansion plans for growth markets	**Contribute to the stability of the financial system** ❯ For more information, see page 51	**Enhance the communities we serve** ❯ For more information, see page 52

performance goals of every business, country and support function are aligned to those of the Group.

Translating the Scorecard across the whole bank takes only four to six weeks. Each section has a scoring mechanism that allows the board to see performance measures. Every six months, the Scorecard is strategically reviewed between Piyush and each MC member. This powerful tool of alignment and execution across the organization is now part of the bank's DNA and is published in its annual report.

Technology Platform

DBS Bank was Building Excellence, but a major issue internally caused concern—technology. Many of its systems were too manual and complicated for their users. Early in the implementation, leaders recognized that the bank's current technology platform and overall technology approach to automate manual processes could not support implementing the DBS House. Not surprising, little investment had been made in technology in 2010. The new implementation required regional standardization, connectivity and a heavy investment in new technology.

"The digital revolution will fundamentally redefine the banking industry in just a few short years."
—Piyush

The bank had already started Process Improvement Events (PIE) before Piyush joined the bank. PIE was an approach for people to redesign a process that needed improving. They would come together for five days to identify the current state, eliminate waste and redesign a future state. On day three of the redesign, the leaders responsible for the process joined to discuss any issues and sign off on what needed to change. They knew what was happening with the process and people needed their buy-in. Due to peer pressure in this setting, it was also hard to say "no."

In 2009, it was decided to conduct five PIEs in the bank. The first—how to reduce credit card applications from a few weeks to two days—was highly successful. On Piyush's first day in the bank, he dropped by a PIE event and immediately recognized the need for conducting more. PIEs gave people the tools to measure, understand and then improve processes.

Customer Service Redesign

From that emerged an aggressive goal to save one million hours internally by eliminating non-value steps and improving the way the bank operated. The goal resulted in a major transformation in people's thinking across the bank that made reaching it about *saving hours* not *cutting costs*. And it was fun!

As PIE became increasingly more successful, the goal of saving one million hours internally was redefined to saving 100 million *customer* hours externally. This paralleled the bank becoming more customer centric. An even greater goal reflected the success of this approach and the amount of change leaders were looking for—that is, set up best-in-class standards that would ensure the bank's targets were better than its competitors.

The barometer moved significantly toward the 100 million mark and with it, employees' belief and confidence grew. They could see their contribution to the DBS House and the roles they played. For example, improving credit card delivery made it easier to do business with the bank, thus providing better service. By 2014, 250 million customer hours had been removed. All measures from the PIEs were confirmed through the CFO office.

During the rollout of PIE, one particular redesign had significant implications. A project was identified to simplify and accelerate the replacement of a credit card after a wallet or purse was lost. When a loss occurred, the customers often would have no cash and couldn't get home. More than that, they worried someone may be using their credit cards, plus they were concerned about the hassle of replacing their lost cards.

After the redesign, the bank acquired feedback from its customers and learned they had created a whole new perspective of the bank's services. Customers thanked the team for making the replacement process easier, and then asked, "But where is my replacement bank card?" This made the team take an even closer look at the whole customer experience.

This redesign shifted the bank's perspective to examining the complete customer journey. The credit card redesign resulted in changed call center scripts and three main realizations. Going forward, they had to:

- treat customers with empathy
- explain the process for replacing all the customer cards
- ask customers if they need any numbers sent via text messaging

By 2013, using automation and analytics had become part of the way things got done in the bank. Measures were established from the system to show performance. Visual management displaying key performance indicators was adopted to show relevant information, ideas and experiments. A coaching program was introduced for leaders on how to leave their offices and converse with members of their staff about making improvements. So was another program to get leaders to constantly think about how to improve processes, not just avoid making mistakes.

Operational Excellence

PIE has since morphed into a program called Operational Excellence across the bank and been incorporated into the culture as "business as usual." The DBS Management System (DMS) has become a mechanism for continuous improvement. DMS coached staff on how to constantly progress and managers on how to drive continuous improvement across their operations. Managers were also trained to have conversations with their people about process improvements while doing "walkabouts" in their business area.

DMS was initiated because, after completing a process improvement, many people did not have the core skills to make continuous improvements. It has also changed the culture of performance. Today, managers do not only receive their bonus when things don't go wrong (as they used to do) but also when they improve a process. These are seen as more than an implementation but as opportunities to solve business problems. And under the "last mile" initiative, every project must clearly stipulate the benefits to the business, stating whether it was useful, useable and used.

Developing the "Heartware"

Although PIE provided the hardware for implementing improvements, the "heartware" was missing. This led to the development of RED in 2011. While PIEs were being conducted, Piyush asked the same team to define the Asian Service pillar in the strategy. The team asked for six weeks but Piyush asked them to take six months. He wanted a launch that had substantial content behind it.

At that time, processes took too long and the bank had big service issues such as long queues at the branches and ATMs. Customers had been queuing up for over an hour in the branch, but the changes made reduced the wait time to less than 15 minutes. Also, from the comfort of their homes, customers can use the bank's apps to check how crowded a branch is and then acquire a queue number via SMS, known as the SMS 'Q'. This system alerts customers when their queue numbers are approaching. In addition, instead of standing in queues, customers can wait their turn more comfortably in chairs.

In addition to talking with customers, the team worked with Singapore Airlines (SIA). The bank identified, for example, how the SIA cabin crew shows respect by kneeling down to speak eye to eye with passengers. Crew members know the names of their priority passengers, no matter where they are sitting in the plane.

As a result of this collaboration, the team came up with 96 ideas about what Asian Service meant. Then in 2011, the top 50 bank leaders spent two days defining Asian Service. This gave birth to the acronym RED, which stands for:

- **R**espectful
- **E**asy to deal with
- **D**ependable

RED made the concept of Asian Service real—something people across the bank could translate into their own work. They were given training to enable them to adopt it in their daily activities. Demonstrating the value of the strategy to the bank, leaders from every country attended a workshop called "Paint Your Goals RED." Also in every country, an Asian Service Implementation Manager

(ASIM) was identified to oversee the adoption of RED, and the RED team reported to the Customer Experience Council (CEC), chaired by Piyush.

In 2010, DBS Bank had the worst service in Singapore as measured independently by the Customer Satisfaction Index of Singapore (CSISG). Four years later, it was rated the best, even higher than SIA. This shows how far the bank has come in the eyes of its customers. Today, RED is used as an adjective in the bank.

Through PIES and RED, employees feel empowered to make changes—and make a difference—driving the customer experience in positive ways.

HCD Thinking and Innovation

The bank's customer-centric approach, which has taken on an integral role in the bank, is moving toward customer journeys and human-centered design (HCD). For example, the bank partnered with LUMA Institute, specialists in innovation, to incorporate HCD thinking into how they design and manage customer journeys from start to end. This practice involves when a customer uses a DBS facility at the branch, ATM or a banking app on a mobile phone. By putting employees in the shoes of customers across a wide spectrum of situations, it allows them to develop a detailed understanding of customers' needs, desires and context to create better experiences.

They also set up a lab to foster HCD thinking and innovation. It's become a facility where different groups of staff can spend time designing and testing concepts before a process is rolled out.

**"Innovation is any new way of doing
things that adds value to the bank."
—Paul Cobban, Chief Operating Officer,
Technology and Operations**

The concept of Asian Innovation was started after Asian Service was introduced in 2011. The initial aim was to create a culture of innovation by teaching people relevant skills so anyone in the bank could innovate.

"Most implementations happen at the side of the businesses. In DBS, it starts with the business issues."
—Neal Cross, Chief Innovation Officer

Most innovation groups in organizations happen at the side of the businesses, creating cool products and solutions and then trying to sell them to companies. They are often rejected because of lack of funding or time. Sometimes egos get in the way.

In DBS Bank, innovation typically starts by asking the business leader, "What is the business problem?" The people involved are taken out for a three-day hackathon, which is a portmanteau of the words "hack" and "marathon." "Hack" is used in the sense of exploratory programming (not illegally breaking into a system) and "thon" refers to a marathon session.

At DBS Bank, a hackathon involves two days of human-centered design and digital training for those involved and three days addressing a real business challenge with outside entities such as startups, entrepreneurs and computer coders. The goal is to invent a prototype solution for the business problem. Interestingly, putting a corporate banker with a startup company is a strange mix that works.

The key learning is how quickly things can be accomplished. Hackathons at DBS were initially designed to invent products, but the bank discovered this was the wrong focus. Rather, they should be used to solve problems and create problem solvers who have been taught the methodology and then to evolve the culture. Talented people from across the bank come together and form teams to focus on a problem and collaboratively develop a solution, all within 72 hours.

A hackathon session translates a problem into a prototype. A Pre-Accelerator (when funding, support and a mentor are provided) then takes the prototype to produce a product, and an Accelerator takes the product to a business. The bank is looking across the entire chain.

From there, all types of experiments are conducted—from creating a mobile app to determining the color of a card a customer prefers. A side benefit is that bank people have learned to say, "Let's experiment on that." In this way, it has changed the culture. People are empowered to experiment and feel unafraid to fail. They know firsthand that something new feels safe when they can test it first.

As mentioned, one of the biggest issues tackled early on was reducing the queue times—as long as 20 minutes—at the ATMs. Adding more ATMs was not a solution; it created more volume as more people used it. They had to find an innovative solution. Adopting human centered design, they observed customers using the ATMs and noted that 40% of the customers don't use the fast cash button even though they're withdrawing the fast cash amount. They observed that people do this so the person behind can't see their balance. When they don't select the fast cash option, they have the choice to request a receipt rather than seeing their balance on the screen.

David Gledhill who heads the Group Technology and Operations area, shared this example: "We used data analytics for forecasting and optimization of cash in our ATMs. We have every single transaction for every single of one of our 1,200 ATMs going to a data warehouse. Now the whole thing is run by a machine. We used to have 400 cashouts (where the ATM ran out of cash) a month. Now the number of cashouts is almost zero. We can predict what demand will be on a Friday night or the night before a public holiday or Chinese New Year. We saved about 300,000 customers a year a wasted trip from going to a machine that was out of cash. That's Asian Service—Dependable."

When the bank moved to its new location in Marina Bay in 2012, a human-centered design lab was established on the 40th floor. Considering the price of real estate in Singapore, this was a significant investment as well as a noteworthy indicator of the bank's intention to understand the customer journey. As David Gledhill said, "A customer's journey encompasses his experience from beginning to end rather than at a single point of transaction. We then adopted human-centered design, a discipline of developing solutions based on our customers' perspective rather than the limitations imposed by our current systems and processes. Human-centered design seeks to answer three questions regarding a journey: 1) Who are our customers and what jobs are they trying to get done? 2) Do we know what they are currently experiencing and saying to others? 3) Do we know how they will respond to our proposed concepts?"

Lab experiments revealed, for example, that 8,000 times a month, people leave their ATM card in the machine despite the visual and audio reminder. They likely get distracted because they're looking at the balance stated on the receipt.

Today, the approach is to identify the business problem, define any risky assumptions and then experiment with a solution by asking questions of the public. Typically, 19 out of 20 assumptions are wrong, but if the problem does get defined correctly, it's a sign to keep going.

The attitude at DBS Bank has become "we have to fail to succeed." People across the organization are able to develop their own ideas rather than have an innovation department push ideas to them. This way, they have greater ownership of their ideas. The term Build Excellence is summed up by Chief Innovation Officer Neal Cross who said, "We want to be as nimble as a startup and embody the culture of a tech company."

Excellence in Execution Challenges
Follow Through

As a leader, how do you know:

- If your execution is progressing forward?
- What is working well?
- What is hindering you?
- How to reinforce the right actions?
- How to create the right conditions for Excellence in Execution?
- How to sustain the execution throughout the implementation journey?
- How often you should you review the execution and to what extent?
- How to encourage more frequent reinforcement across the organization?
- How often you should appraise your people?

Language of Execution: hackathon, check-ins, self-directed, recognition and reward, snowball effect, CEM, Review Rhythm

Materials featured in this book are available at www.implementation-hub.com/tools_tips_techniques/excellence-in-execution

Follow Through

 Video Quiz: When your salary reaches $75,000, what starts to happen?

*F*ollow Through is the last area to be discussed, but in some organizations, it is the first. For example, in a Singapore healthcare company I worked with, the new CEO had inherited a failed execution from his predecessor. He used this to his advantage by starting the execution with a review of what had previously gone wrong. He engaged not only leaders but people at all levels of the organization for their opinions. When he started the new transformation, he had gathered valuable feedback and also galvanized a high level of support because people perceived him as open and willing to listen.

Follow Through is the number one best practice of leaders in organizations that are Excellent in Execution.

In the Follow Through phase, leaders constantly check and make sure what was agreed on was acted on, the right outcomes were achieved and people were recognized for their contribution. They know if they don't frequently reinforce employees' contributions, the actions won't be sustained and people won't feel inspired to keep participating. They will likely slip back into doing what they were doing before the launch of the strategy.

Execution is only sustained when you reward and recognize individuals for taking the right actions.

When Lou Gerstner took over as CEO of IBM, he saw signs promoting teamwork everywhere. But when he checked how people were paid, he discovered it was based on individual performance, not teamwork. He immediately set about adjusting the IBM reward system to support group efforts.

When James Kilts took over as CEO of Gillette, the organization had missed its earnings estimates for the previous 15 consecutive quarters. Kitts was surprised to discover that, despite this poor performance, most of the leaders had been rated high in their performances and received maximum bonuses. Kilts went about changing the structure from being rewarded for *effort* to being rewarded for *performance*. Like Gerstner, he set about ensuring the reinforcement aligned with the stated strategy objectives.

Powerful Execution Tip: As people take the right actions, find ways to reinforce the desired behavior going forward.

There's a realistic risk that your organization's performance will decline if people don't receive the right reinforcement. This is because they may feel rejected and dejected by the lack of reinforcement, and thus they contribute less.

Powerful Execution Tip: Make achieving strategic objectives part of the leaders' bonus.

> **To demonstrate the importance of a project and its value, link its successful completion to people's bonus. Make sure the more important the project, the higher percentage of bonus is assigned.**

The End of Annual Appraisals

In at least 10% of Fortune 500 organizations, annual appraisals have been abandoned. Why? Leaders can no longer wait 12 months before sitting down with employees to discuss their performance.

Annual appraisals are also expensive and mostly ineffective. So taking a different approach can create a tremendous opportunity to not only sustain the execution but be more cost-effective.

For example, an employee is involved in a hackathon and created an idea for a new app that improves the customer interface. The app moves forward into an incubator and within 90 days, a prototype is developed. This type of activity can recur multiple times in a year. Reviewing the employee's performance only once a year isn't timely enough to capture and appreciate a person's contribution. Once a quarter is recommended.

> **The accelerated pace of transformation means that within 90-day blocks of time, more is happening than ever before. Check in with your people at least once a quarter.**

Globoforce reported that 53% of employees say reviews don't motivate them to work harder and that 71% want feedback ASAP. [92] In fact, annual appraisals can be more disruptive than value adding. In addition to being time-consuming, they can foster mistrust between employees and their boss, and they are often seen as unfair. Deloitte calculated the time spent preparing for annual

92 http://www.globoforce.com/gfblog/2013/infographic-the-startling-truth-about-performance-reviews

appraisals and conducting them, noting around two million hours a year were devoted to annual performance appraisals.[93]

Here's how more companies weighed in on this:

- Microsoft abandoned appraisals because leaders believed they restricted collaboration and creativity.[94]
- Accenture abandoned its annual appraisals for its 330,000 employees because leaders observed the appraisals were demotivating.[95]
- GE followed suit also in 2015. The organization that, under Jack Welch, introduced the "rank and yank" system (GE used the bell curve and fired those who performed at the bottom 10%) adopted a process focused on employees' goals rather than on their grades. GE leaders recognized the need for more regular "touchpoints" with its employees. (Touchpoints are informal checks to set priorities so organizations can respond faster to changes.) Compare this to waiting a year under the Employee Management System, which is being phased out.[96]

Powerful Execution Tip: Annual appraisals are often irrelevant, demotivating and too late to inspire employees. If you have not already, consider abandoning them in your organization in favor of quarterly "check-ins."

Leaders need to change the review conversation as employees become more self-directed. Check-ins shift the conversation from past to future and from managing employees to encouraging higher performance and engagement through the right feedback.

---

93   https://hbr.org/2015/04/reinventing-performance-management
94   http://fortune.com/2015/10/29/microsoft-dell-performance-reviews/
95   https://www.washingtonpost.com/news/on-leadership/wp/2015/07/21/in-big-move-accenture-will-get-rid-of-annual-performance-reviews-and-rankings/
96   http://qz.com/428813/ge-performance-review-strategy-shift/

Self-Directed Individuals in Today's Organizations

Employees are more self-directed than ever. In some organizations, only 20% of them have fixed positions and the remaining 80% move from one project to the next. Their work is evaluated at the end of each project. Like actors working on a movie, they throw all their energy and talent into the current project. As soon as it's complete, they transfer that energy and talent to their next movie.

This represents a dramatic change to the management approach in the second half of the 20th century, which was heavily influenced by World War II. In that era, managers gave orders and employees carried out those orders—a command and control approach.

In the 21st century, the transition from managers to leaders emphasizes that people respond more to guidance and coaching than a command and control approach. They're also becoming more self-directed in these ways:

- Employees don't depend on the organization for training and development because they leverage what's available outside of work. This includes doing research and taking courses online.
- They are empowered to make changes as organizations become more agile and the ecosystem is built to support them.
- They are working cross-functionally in teams and across borders.
- They may have more than one boss.

To check on what team members are doing, team leaders meet regularly with them, either in person or on conference calls—to share feedback, learn about progress being made and determine where they may need support.

Powerful Execution Tip: Provide feedback to employees as soon as possible along the implementation journey.

Self-Directed People

To encourage employees to be self-directed, consider taking these actions:

- ✓ **Show appreciation.** Inspire your people.
- ✓ **Set up a coaching structure.** Assist people to improve.
- ✓ **Make it brief.** Plan feedback sessions to last about 30 minutes.
- ✓ **Provide frequent feedback.** Structure a minimum of four feedback sessions a year and allow for ad hoc meetings as required. Always show appreciation when appropriate.
- ✓ **Be sincere and authentic.** Employees will abandon the system if they even sense insincerity. If you are too busy, then postpone a meeting rather than rushing through it. Don't say your door is always open if you don't demonstrate it. Being sincere will build trust and quality relationships.
- ✓ **Make sure people get paid enough.** This helps ensure money is not an issue in performing their work.

Numerous surveys conclude that employees tend to receive negative feedback immediately but rarely get positive feedback right away. Positive feedback not only results in people being more engaged but also encourages them to develop their skills faster. In addition, frequent dialog creates a better relationship between an employee and his or her immediate boss.

Reinforcement includes both rewards (the financial contribution) and recognition (nonfinancial). Both aspects need to be considered to achieve Excellence in Execution. It can't succeed without reinforcing the right actions throughout the implementation journey.

Providing the Right Feedback

According to Sheila Heen, co-author of *Thanks for the Feedback*,[97] employees require three types of feedback: appreciation, coaching and evaluation.

---

97 http://www.amazon.com/Thanks-Feedback-Science-Receiving-Well/dp/0670014664

Appreciation

Appreciation is a form of encouragement that shows employees their contribution is recognized. It can be as straightforward as a simple "thank you." Many leaders believe money is the number one motivator of people at work, but in most situations, it is not. Instead, receiving the right kind of appreciation at the right time inspires people. Employees pay attention to what gets reinforced more than what is said. They also share with each other about the recognition they receive.

As a leader, reinforcing the right actions of your people assists you to:

- Align the performance to the strategy
- Sustain momentum along the implementation journey
- Recognize contributors and top performers so they (especially the early adopters) participate in the execution and feel encouraged to continue
- Send the right messages throughout the organization

Coaching

As a coach, a leader's role to create meaningful goals, guide people to achieve those goals, assist when obstacles need to be overcome and celebrate successes.

Coaching to improve performance can be informal on-the-job coaching or structured with a business coach. The structured approach is often adopted when someone is being groomed for promotion or has an issue in the workplace. In sports, the best performers in the world have coaches. However, at work, being appointed a coach is often perceived as a negative intervention when it's not.

Evaluation

Leaders need to regularly evaluate the person's performance in a fair way. Each evaluation should clarify decisions and aim to manage expectations.

Appreciation can inspire us, coaching can assist us to improve and evaluation can tell us how we are doing.

Debunking a Belief: Money is the Number One Motivator

In my book *Bricks to Bridges* I presented that, for many organizations, reinforcement initiatives are badly designed and ineffective because they're based on assuming that money is the number one motivator of people for business. This is not true. Money is a "hygiene" requirement and not a motivator. *Not* having money is a demotivating factor. But once people have enough to satisfy their needs (based on Maslow's Hierarchy of Needs), the importance of money declines. When I first presented this in 2004, it was often challenged. However, since then new research noted here now supports this argument.

> **"Money motivates neither the best people**
> **nor the best in people. Purpose does."**
> **—Nilofer Merchan, business innovator**

Powerful Execution Tip: People take the right actions when they have the right incentives. What incentives are you using and are they having the desired effect?

AON, a business consultancy focused on risk, insurance and people, contends that, at best, monetary compensation can only be a "non-negative." That means if you pay too little, you will fail to gain engagement and not attract the right people. If you overpay, the effect is *not* the opposite. You get neither overwork nor engagement because other factors drive employee motivation.

A study[98] conducted at Massachusetts Institute of Technology and funded by the U.S. Federal Reserve Bank revealed many surprising findings. It demonstrated that, for straightforward tasks without much cognitive application, money motivated the worker. However, as soon as cognitive application was required, paying people more actually had a startling effect on their performance. A larger reward led to poorer performance!

---

98   http://www.fiercegovernmentit.com/story/mit-discovers-secret-human-motivation-money/2011-11-16

Other research published since I noted this in *Bricks to Bridges* includes the following:

- *Forbes Magazine:* In the 2010 article "Money Is Not The Best Motivator" by Jon R. Katzenbach and Zia Khan, the authors argue that people are inspired by having autonomy, but more money doesn't often equal greater perceived autonomy. [99]
- A 2010 Harvard study by Teresa M. Amabile and Steven J. Kramer examined the day-to-day activities, emotions and motivation levels of hundreds of knowledge workers in a wide variety of settings.[100] They concluded that the number one motivator for people at work was *progress*—that is, feeling they were moving forward and achieving a greater goal. "When workers sense they're making headway, their drive to succeed is at its peak," the article stated.
- *McKinsey Quarterly:* In a 2009 article "Motivating people: Getting beyond money" by Martin Dewhurst, Matthew Guthridge and Elizabeth Mohr, the authors argued that three noncash motivators—praise from immediate managers, leadership attention and a chance to lead projects or task forces—are no less effective motivators (or even more) than the three highest-rated financial incentives: cash bonuses, increased base pay and stock or stock options.[101]

Powerful Execution Tip: Money is the most expensive way to motivate people, so identify other options you can use.

Another argument why money is not a good motivator lies in answering the question, "Is enough money ever enough?" To many people's surprise, the answer is "yes."

99 http://www.forbes.com/2010/04/06/money-motivation-pay-leadership-managing-employees.html
100 https://hbr.org/2010/01/the-hbr-list-breakthrough-ideas-for-2010/ar/1
101 http://www.mckinsey.com/business-functions/organization/our-insights/motivating-people-getting-beyond-money

There is no measurable happiness difference between people earning, for example, $75,000 a year and those earning $250,000. Research supporting this was conducted at Princeton University's Woodrow Wilson School in 2010[102] and articles were published in *Forbes*[103] and the *Wall Street Journal*.[104] Researchers at Randstad[105] claim that 36% of employees would give up $5,000 a year in salary to be happier at work.

Yet in many organizations, the reinforcement program is primarily structured around money as a motivator—a flawed design in most situations. These programs should be about inspiring and engaging your people by providing purposeful work.

More money does not mean more happiness. Happiness starts maxing out once you earn around $75,000 and survival needs are satisfied. *This is the answer to the video quiz.*

Why Awards Work Better than Money

For people doing creative work, awards inspire more than money for reasons such as these:

- Symbolic awards send a more powerful message than giving cash, and they are also discussed among peers.
- Awards associated with a specific execution action can elevate the importance of the action in the eyes of employees.
- Cash disappears through paying bills, taxi fares and so on, thus leaving no symbolic and lasting benefit.
- Awards are not interpreted as a taxable benefit; money is taxable.
- Awards can be personalized to the individual; cash is impersonal.

---

102 http://content.time.com/time/magazine/article/0,9171,2019628,00.html
103 http://www.forbes.com/sites/learnvest/2012/04/24/the-salary-that-will-make-you-happy-hint-its-less-than-75000
104 http://blogs.wsj.com/wealth/2010/09/07/the-perfect-salary-for-happiness-75000-a-year
105 http://www.randstad.com.sg/about-randstad/our-research

- The value of a noncash award is increased by what it represents—that is, awards can have a lower financial value than a cash payment yet provide the same or greater prestige and motivation.

Three Elements for Taking the Right Actions

An interesting piece of research for reinforcing execution actions comes from Stanford University's Persuasive Technology Lab. Dr. BJ Fogg has developed the Fogg Behavior Model (FBM)[106] in which he sets out three main elements required for an individual to feel inspired. They are:

1. Motivation
2. Ability
3. Trigger

"The model asserts that for a target behavior to happen, a person must have sufficient motivation, sufficient ability, and an effective trigger. All three factors must be present at the same instant for the behavior to occur."
—BJ Fogg, researcher

Let's examine each of these elements and their implication to the implementation journey.

1. Motivation

Motivation is a person's desire to achieve results. Individuals won't take action if they're not inspired to do so. Fogg describes three core motivators that all have two sides:

- Pleasure/Pain—Either pain or pleasure is associated with an action.
- Hope/Fear—It's anticipated an outcome will be either good or bad.
- Social Acceptance/Rejection—People are inspired to do what will win them social acceptance and avoid what will not.

---

106 www.bjfogg.com

What is the implication of these motivators for an implementation journey? At the launch of the strategy, the CEO and the leadership team explain the benefits of executing the new strategy while highlighting the pleasure of participating. Individuals also want to know how the execution will affect them. Will there be any pain such as losing their jobs? Will they have more responsibility or less?

2. Ability

How easy is it for the person to take the desired actions? Consider these six elements:

- Time—If we don't have the time, then we don't have the ability.
- Money—If the action requires money we don't have, then we have a problem.
- Physical Effort—When this is required, it may make changing harder.
- Brain Cycles—We have more ability to perform a behavior that is not mentally fatiguing versus one that is.
- Social Deviance—If it goes against the norm, then the action is harder to take.
- Non-Routine—It is hard to break habits.

What is the implication of these elements for an implementation journey? The leaders are responsible for giving people the ability to execute. They can do so if they:

- Eliminate work that's no longer value adding.
- Provide the budget to support the new strategy.
- Encourage and inspire additional effort.
- Create the space for individuals to discuss and reflect on the implementation.
- Make it socially acceptable to participate.
- Encourage individuals to break old habits and adopt the new strategy.

3. Trigger

A trigger is the call to action that could be an email, an alarm or a mobile message. Without a trigger, the target action simply won't happen.

Fogg identifies three types of triggers:

- Spark as Trigger—This is when individuals lack motivation and need to be inspired.
- Facilitator as Trigger—This is appropriate for people who have high motivation but lack ability.
- Signal as Trigger—This reminder works well when people have both ability and motivation.

What is the implication of the trigger for an implementation journey? The role of a leader is to be the spark that encourages and facilitates individuals to take the right action. Through discussions, the leader breaks down how employees are expected to participate in the strategy. They conduct regular reviews with individuals after actions have been taken. To watch Dr Fogg present his model in a fast, easy way, go to: https://www.youtube.com/watch?v=jsbF9z6adAo.

Powerful Execution Tip: You can publish positive statements and say all the right things, but if you promote people who take the wrong actions, the resulting cynicism can derail your efforts. Ensure your people are recognized for the right reasons.

How can leaders know when to recognize employees and ensure the execution is progressing well? They conduct regular execution reviews.

Conduct Regular Execution Reviews

When leaders leverage reinforcement correctly, regular reviews sustain the execution.

Executing the strategy requires moving from theory to practice, from concept to conceptualization and from formulation to execution. Reviews support success by making small but often critical corrections along the way. These corrections have a disproportional effect on the outcomes. It's like when astronauts fly a spaceship to the moon; the smallest correction can make the difference between landing on the moon and completely missing it. Along the way, astronauts have to check the spaceship's location in outer space relative to where it's heading. Similarly, you check your organization's location on the implementation journey relative to its strategy objectives.

Unbelievably, many leaders don't conduct reviews frequently enough. As a result, by the time they do check on progress, it can be too late to get back on track. Small problems can snowball into large problems, creating a snowball effect.

There are few absolutes in business, but as noted earlier, *whatever you discuss and plan when designing your strategy changes during its execution.* Therefore, adjustments must be made to account for changes, such as in customer expectations, products, market conditions, employees and measures. Also, no one knows the exact steps to take along the journey, so constantly reviewing what you expected compared to what's happening is critical.

Excellence in Execution demands conducting regular reviews.

The only way you know a strategy is good or bad is by executing, testing and reviewing it. Yet Bridges' 2016 survey revealed that almost 50% of organizations review their strategy execution fewer than three times a year, while only one in five review it once a month.[107]

To predict where an organization will be in two or three years, Excellence in Execution requires regularly examining the strategy and the actions taken. This involves having the discipline to ask people how they are doing *every week*, stepping back to examine different part of the execution *every two weeks*, reviewing the whole execution *every quarter* and gathering everyone to discuss the journey *every year*. This approach sustains the execution and ensures people are not only talking about it but also acting on it.

---

107 http://www.implementation-hub.com/resources/implementation-surveys

Powerful Execution Tip: Create a culture in which strategy check-ins become a habit, just like employee check-ins.

Many leaders say they don't have time for another meeting or review. However, strategy execution reviews are not just another meeting; they guide the future of the organization. So a better question to ask is this: "Can you afford *not* to meet on a regular basis to know how the future of the organization is progressing?"

Examples of Check-Ins

In their book *Leading Culture Change in Global Organizations,* Daniel Denison, Robert Hooijberg, Nancy Lane and Colleen Lief shared a story about how the leaders of the candy-making company Mars held a two-day meeting.[108] The first morning, the meeting was held in Prague. After lunch, the team boarded a bus to Budapest where they met for the second day. Why waste time travelling to a second city?

Along the way, the bus stopped at numerous stores so the leadership team could check how well their products were positioned on the shop shelves. This powerfully demonstrated how the organization's strategy is executed in the field while reinforcing what was important. Clearly, it was more important to physically review the product placement with the leaders than to just discuss it in a meeting room.

In another example with an airline client, I was invited at the start of our relationship to join the steering committee meetings. I observed that the biweekly leadership meetings were completely focused on operations, while any strategy and its execution weren't even discussed. I knew that changing the agenda alone was not enough. Even though the execution review was added at the request of the CEO, it was the last item on the agenda and was rushed. Why this focus on operations? Because leaders were only being held accountable for quarterly performance.

---

108 Daniel Denison, Robert Hooijberg, Nancy Lane and Colleen Lief, *Leading Culture Change in Global Organizations: Aligning Culture and Strategy.* Jossey-Bass, 2012. p. 49.

I recommended a separate biweekly execution meeting to complement the traditional leadership meeting. It meant team members had to create more time to meet and prepare, but the increased effort was necessary to meet the execution goals. The CEO chaired the meetings and made sure progress was discussed in detail. The two separate meetings ran for about 18 months. After that, the CEO consolidated them once the discipline of reviewing the execution had been instilled into the leadership and the organization.

> *Powerful Execution Tip*: Distinguish execution reviews from regular operational reviews. If required, separate the two.

In another example, a CEO held his regular operational reviews at a rectangular table. There, he expected his managers to represent the interests of their business. However, he held strategic reviews at a round table where he expected everyone to discuss what was best for the whole organization. The physical move to the round table reinforced that everyone had to contribute to the strategy and its execution. It conveyed that each person's input was important.

Reviews to improve performance can also take the form of checklists. Johns Hopkins University impressively reduced its hospital infection rate from 4% to nil by adopting a five-step checklist in its intensive care unit.[109] This checklist reminded doctors to take the key actions. In Dr Fogg's language, the checklist was a trigger.

Strategy Put Front and Center

Conducting regular reviews also changes the dialog in the organization and specifically in meetings. They focus people on the strategy *and* its execution— what it promises, how to adopt it, what actions to take, why it's important, what's working and what's not.

To change the dialog, a question to ask is this: "What have you done this week to execute the strategy?" By asking this question at the start of every meeting, the leader puts the strategy and its execution where it should be, front

---

109 http://psqh.com/preventing-healthcare-associated-infections

and center. And remember, individuals pay attention to what their immediate boss pays attention to.

If you as a leader don't pay attention to the execution, then neither will your people.

 ### Benefits of Structured Reviews

Establishing structured, regular reviews as a discipline is a best practice of Excellence in Execution organizations. It comes with these benefits:

✓ Demonstrates that the strategy and its execution are important across the organization
✓ Cascades the right messages down through the organization
✓ Reminds and reinforces the strategy objectives
✓ Ensures the right actions are being taken
✓ Keeps the execution on the leaders' radar
✓ Allows for critical adjustments sooner rather than later
✓ Identifies upstream changes to the strategy
✓ Holds people accountable
✓ Keeps the execution on track
✓ Makes execution a habit
✓ Encourages organizational learning
✓ Provides an opportunity to celebrate success

Focus on the Positive

When you look at the diagram below, what do you notice?

- $1 \times 1 = 1$
- $2 \times 2 = 4$
- $3 \times 3 = 9$
- $4 \times 4 = 14$

Most people focus on the 4X4 being wrong, not that 75% of the diagram is correct. In strategy execution, plenty goes wrong and leaders need to praise what is right as well as correct what is wrong.

Review Rhythm for Checking Progress

Most leaders don't spend enough time reviewing the execution, yet reviews are one of the most important activities for achieving Excellence in Execution. Bridges' latest research revealed that 85% of organizations spend less than 10 hours a month discussing their execution.[110]

So how often should you review strategy execution? I suggest leaders ask their people every week what they're doing to contribute to the execution. Then every two weeks, they conduct reviews in each business vertical to examine different components of the execution. That way, by the end of every quarter, they have a complete assessment of the execution progress. Then they would review the overall performance once a year.

It takes discipline to change the dialog across an organization. Leaders are responsible for creating the space for the reviews first on their own calendars. Commonly, they find this difficult because they get swept along by the current of everyday activities.

Sharing Bad News, Too

In 2006, Alan Mulally became CEO of Ford during an extremely difficult time. The organization was on the brink of bankruptcy. By the time he left in 2014, he had turned it around.

When the organization was struggling, Mulally introduced the discipline of daily reviews to identify problems before they snowballed. He encouraged leaders to be open, to support each other and to nurture personal accountability. The daily reviews shifted the culture of the meetings. For example, in Mulally's early meetings, all the reports showed the data in green (positive), yet the organization was losing millions. This was because the leaders were afraid to share the bad news. They were also concerned about their colleagues taking advantage of their

---

110 http://www.implementation-hub.com/resources/implementation-surveys

poor performance. Mulally insisted the reviews be correct; by doing so, he could start to successfully transform Ford.

> *Powerful Execution Tip*: Successful strategy execution requires a rigorous confrontation of reality in your reviews. Ensure you are asking penetrating questions and don't avoid the tough discussions.

Keeping the review meetings short and succinct is also required. Convening for more than two hours is a workshop, not a meeting. As an example, Amazon CEO Jeff Bezos insists that anyone who calls a meeting provides a three-page briefing on the objectives of the meeting and the content for discussion. Participants then spend the first 20 minutes of an hour-long meeting reading the notes and the remaining 40 minutes discussing the points.

As a leader, you need to encourage sharing bad news as well as good news across the organization or you aren't obtaining the full picture. Excellence for Execution includes encouraging people to share any bad news while ensuring them it's not a CEM (Career Ending Move).

"Sometimes, I think my most important job as a CEO is to listen for bad news. If you don't act on it, your people will eventually stop bringing bad news to your attention and that is the beginning of the end."
—Bill Gates, former CEO, Microsoft

Adopt a Review Rhythm

Conducting regular reviews creates the Review Rhythm—a pattern and expectation that progress is checked. It also balances the strategy and operations conversation and overcomes the execution juxtaposition challenge discussed earlier.

Excellence in Execution organizations adopt the Review Rhythm indicated in Figure 14.1:

Figure 14.1

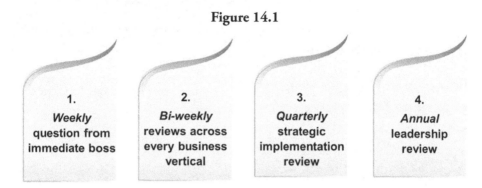

1.	2.	3.	4.
Weekly question from immediate boss	*Bi-weekly* reviews across every business vertical	*Quarterly* strategic implementation review	*Annual* leadership review

Weekly questions from an immediate boss demonstrate not only the importance of the strategy being executed but also taking the right actions. It tells people they'll be asked how they are progressing against the actions they plan to take, and it allows for support and coaching.

Biweekly reviews across business verticals ensure people in the organization have the discipline and are taking the right actions. It allows for immediate corrective action and support such as allocating resources and reinforcing the right actions.

Quarterly strategic implementation reviews (called SIR by Bridges) involve the top leaders and invited employees. They encapsulate the discussions and actions from the biweekly reviews across all the business verticals and provide a summary of the progress being made throughout the organization. They also might identify flaws in the strategy that need correcting as they collectively examine the feedback from the biweekly reviews.

Annual leadership reviews set aside a time to reflect on performance, share best practices, define lessons learned and embed changes. They bring together the key players in the execution and present opportunities to celebrate successes.

What you ask in the review dramatically affects the actions taken by your people and the success of your execution.

In your reviews, do you pay more attention to short-term performance than on the strategy execution? If you focus more on short-term performance, you're creating a strategic juxtaposition. To avoid that, use the recommended questions in Figure 14.2 to guide you through the Review Rhythm.

Figure 14.2

1.	2.	3.	4.
Weekly question from immediate boss	*Bi-weekly* reviews across every business vertical	*Quarterly* strategic implementation review	*Annual* leadership review

Weekly	Biweekly	Quarterly	Annual
What have you done this week to execute the strategy?	Which strategic objectives are you focused on and what actions are you taking to execute them?	What have we done in the last 90 days to execute the strategy?	What have we achieved in the past 12 months?
Is the work you're currently doing adding value to the new strategy?	What mistakes have been made that we can learn from?	Have we provided the right resources?	What has changed in our strategy and what is the impact on the execution?
Are the actions you're taking today driving the execution forward?	From the Strategy Scorecard, which measures are performing well and what concerns are outstanding?	Are people taking the right actions to deliver the strategic objectives we are currently focused on?	What mistakes did we make?
What support do you need to succeed?	What should we stop doing?	What are our successes?	What lessons have we learned?

Weekly	Biweekly	Quarterly	Annual
	What are we doing right?	What should we stop doing?	What more can we do to support our people?
	What is being communicated about the execution?	What assumptions have we made and were they accurate?	What was successful that we should keep doing?
	What are our recent successes?	What has changed in our strategic landscape?	What are the best practices we can share?
	What support do you need to succeed?	What can we do to be more effective as a team?	What can we celebrate?
	What needs to change in our current approach to the execution?	What needs to change in our approach?	
	When we meet again for our next review, what key achievement(s) will you aim to share?	When we meet again for our next review, what key achievement(s) will you aim to share?	

The review records any changes to the execution including:

- Additions—What new action steps need to be taken?
- Deletions—What should we stop doing?
- Amendments—What are the changes to current actions?
- Assumptions—Are any assumptions we've made still relevant?

Powerful Execution Tip: It's important to frame the review question the right way. Don't ask, "Why did you not tell me there was a problem." Instead ask, "What was the issue that caused the target to be missed?"

SAF Example

Singapore Air Force (SAF) recently leveraged its regular reviews to change the culture around fighter jet near misses. Previously, near misses were not encouraged to be reported as the culture did not want to know. The head of the Singapore Air Force changed this because it contradicted the organization's strategic focus of embedding safety as a discipline.

Today, SAF takes the following steps when a near miss occurs:

- Everyone in SAF is informed, and both bad and good news are shared.
- The focus is not on the *individual* but on the *incident* so others can learn from it.
- Measures are in place to track key actions.
- The ground crew and air crew alike know the importance of reporting near misses.
- Every quarter, the chief attends the safety forum to discuss, review and make positive changes to avoid future incidents.

Similarly, you can adjust the format and questions in your meetings to change the dialog across the whole organization.

Sample Template for Conducting a Review

The template below includes different sections. All or just some can be used.

1. Action Items Review

A review highlights what has been achieved in the last 90 days and the results of the execution to date against the strategic objectives. Presenters explain:

- The actions taken
- The impact of the actions
- Challenges that have arisen
- How people have approached or dealt with the challenges

Questions for discussion:

- What are the key deliverables of the strategy people have been working on?
- What is the progress against the execution timeline?
- What measures have shifted (negatively or positively)?
- What needs to be done differently?
- Are we holding people accountable?
- What needs to change in our approach?
- What major milestones have been achieved to date?
- What can we celebrate?

2. Strategic Landscape Review

This is an opportunity to step back and review the macro perspective by asking, "What significant trends have impacted the strategy and/or the execution?" This question has increased in importance as BMD (Business Model Disruption) becomes more frequent. Areas to consider include:

- Customer trends
- Competition changes
- Innovations
- Market conditions
- Geopolitical shifts
- Organizational changes
- Environmental analysis

Consider using or revisiting Porters Five Forces:

- Threat of new competition
- Threat of substitute products or services
- Bargaining power of customers (buyers)
- Bargaining power of suppliers
- Intensity of competitive rivalry

3. Critical Success Factors (CSF) Assessment

The CSF assessment establishes the key drivers and challenges that will make or break the execution. Review the CSFs to identify any impending changes and ask these discussion questions:

- What are the CSFs for the strategy execution?
- Are they still relevant?
- How is the organization performing against them?

4. Organizational Learning

The key lessons learned during the execution need to be documented and discussed. Doing this builds on the CSFs and ensures organizational learning takes place so mistakes aren't repeated and best practices are adopted.

Consider these questions for discussion:

- What key lessons have been learned about the challenges of implementing the strategy in the last 90 days?
- What do we need to do differently as a result of these lessons?
- What do we need to adopt to avoid repeating mistakes?
- What do we need to capture to ensure we learn the best practices?

5. Next Steps

Changes to the plans for execution are recorded as:

- Additions
- Deletions
- Changes

When a new action is created, new owners of the action and delivery dates are established for each.

A best practice is to send or post a summary of the outcomes from reviews to relevant parties within 24 hours of completing them.

Another best practice is to invite key people in the execution (from the frontline or middle managers) to sit in on the reviews. This provides them with the opportunity and exposure to observe the leadership meeting.

Among the eight areas for Excellence in Execution that make up the Implementation Compass, Review is the least practiced by leaders around the world. Individuals service their car and go for personal health checkups regularly; organizations scan their computers for viruses routinely. But do they regularly check to ensure their executions are on course?

To achieve Excellence in Execution, conducting regular reviews is a must.

Chapter Fifteen

Questions to Build HOW (Part Three)

To encourage the right actions and sustain the execution, regular reinforcement and reviews are required to Follow Through. Leaders in organizations that are Excellent in Execution understand that Follow Through is the number one best practice.

Execution is only sustained when people are rewarded and recognized for taking the right actions. Leaders often do many things right and then skip over the reinforcement. As a result, people stop being engaged because they feel rejected and dejected.

HOW Questions to Follow Through

For leaders, today's accelerated pace means checking in on their people more frequently, providing feedback and measuring people's performance against the strategic objectives. As a leader, you ask these questions:

1. Do we need to review people's performance more frequently than we currently do?

To encourage employees to be more self-directed, ask:

2. Is the organization creating the right learning conditions in which people can select their own training in skills required to execute the strategy?
3. Are people empowered so the organization can be agile?
4. Is the structure of the organization supportive and able to achieve Excellence in Execution?

Providing feedback to your people is no longer based on assessing past performance but on future performance. Feedback involves providing appreciation, coaching and evaluation. To know if you're achieving that, consider asking these questions:

5. Do people feel appreciated by their immediate supervisor?
6. Is coaching available to those who *want* it as well as those who *need* it?
7. Do people regularly receive evaluations that fairly assess their performance?
8. Is the feedback conducted in 30 minutes or less?
9. Are leaders and supervisors trained to provide authentic feedback?

Providing reinforcement regularly results in people being more self-directed and engaged. However, reinforcement programs are often flawed because they are structured around money as the primary motivator. Money is the most expensive motivator and, in many jobs, not the best one. People need to have a clear line of sight between the new actions they're taking and the reinforcement they're receiving. Therefore, to build and sustain Excellence in Execution, design a program that provides positive support around the right actions.

In many organizations, reviews focus mostly on day-to-day operations with the execution checked only every six months or annually. This is not frequent enough; small problems escalate during that time.

Establishing structured regular reviews is a disciplined best practice because it gives support while reinforcing key messages and objectives. It also ensures the right actions are taken, allows for changes, holds people accountable and identifies opportunities to celebrate.

To determine if reviews are effective, ask these questions:

10. Do the reviews resonate through the organization and demonstrate the importance of the execution?
11. Are reviews cascading the right messages down through the organization?
12. Do they ensure the right actions are being taken?
13. Is the execution on every leader's radar?
14. Are necessary adjustments being made?
15. Are people being held accountable?
16. Are the reviews keeping the execution on track?
17. Is execution becoming a productive habit in the organization? *Organizations adopt different habits but not all of them are good.*
18. Do reviews encourage organizational learning? *Reviews should be seen as an opportunity for the organization to grow.*
19. Do they create an opportunity to celebrate successes?

Some leaders have difficulty finding the time for execution, so ask this question:

20. Can you afford *not* to meet regularly to know how the future of the organization is progressing?

Each week, leaders ask their people what they are doing to contribute to the execution. Every two weeks, leaders in each business vertical examine the different components of the execution. Every quarter, they complete an overall assessment of the execution progress and once a year, they review the overall performance.

Questions to ask weekly include:

21. What have you done this week to execute the strategy? *People are asked this by their immediate boss.*

22. Is the work you're doing adding value to the new strategy? *This tests the employee's understanding of the strategy and its objectives.*
23. Are the actions you're taking today driving the execution forward? *This encourages a clear line of sight between an employee's actions and the strategy objectives.*
24. What support do you need to succeed?

Questions to ask biweekly include:

25. Which strategic objectives are you focused on and what actions are you taking to execute them?
26. What mistakes has the organization made that can be learned from?
27. From the Strategy Scorecard, what measures are performing well?
28. From the Strategy Scorecard, what concerns are showing up?
29. What should the organization stop doing? *This is just as important as asking what it should start doing.*
30. What is the organization doing right?
31. What is being communicated about the execution?
32. What are the organization's recent successes?
33. What support do people need to succeed?
34. What needs to change in the execution approach?
35. In the next review, what key achievement(s) will you aim to share?

Questions to ask quarterly include:

36. What has the organization done in the last 90 days to execute the strategy?
37. Has the organization provided the right resources?
38. Are people taking the right actions to deliver the strategic objectives the organization is currently focused on?
39. What are the organization's successes?
40. Are leaders being transparent and authentic throughout the journey?

41. What assumptions have the organization's leaders made and were they accurate?
42. What has changed in the organization's strategic landscape?
43. What can the organization do to be more effective as a team?
44. What needs to change in the execution approach?
45. In the next review, what key achievement(s) will you aim to share?

Questions to ask annually include:

46. What has the organization achieved in the past 12 months?
47. What has changed in the strategy and how does that affect the execution?
48. What mistakes have been made?
49. What lessons have been learned?
50. Are the lessons learned being shared across the organization?
51. What more can leaders in the organization do to support people?
52. What was successful that the organization should keep doing?
53. What are the best practices the organization should share?
54. What successes can be celebrated?

During the reviews, focus on the positives as well as what can be improved. Also make sure review meetings don't exceed two hours and encourage people to share both bad news and good news.

Conducting regular reviews of the overall execution will ensure that day-to-day activity doesn't swallow up the future. In fact, the odds of successfully executing a strategy that isn't reviewed frequently are slim to none.

Chapter Sixteen

DBS Case Study Follow Through

*H*aving recognized the need to support and encourage the right actions to implement the DBS House, the bank's leaders developed a new performance management system in 2011. Managers were trained in the system, which helped make the strategy real for people across as the bank. The system was linked to the Scorecard and allowed for teams who demonstrated the right actions to earn a bonus.

The three main thrusts of new system were to:

1. **Pay for performance measured against the balanced Scorecard.** This created a pay-for-performance culture across the bank. In turn, it ensured a close link between total compensation and the annual and long-term business objectives as measured through the Scorecard. It also emphasized the importance of how goals were achieved, and it brought in the PRIDE! values.

2. **Provide market-competitive pay.** Employee compensation was benchmarked against other organizations of similar size and standing for fairness. This ensured the top talent in the bank was compensated against the upper quartile (or higher) in the market.

3. **Guard against excessive risk-taking.** Leaders focused on achieving risk-adjusted returns consistent with its prudent risk and capital management. They also placed an emphasis on long-term sustainable outcomes and aligned incentive payments with the long-term performance of the bank through deferral and claw-back arrangements.

The new performance management system included 360-degree appraisals. In addition, several ways of encouraging the right actions were put in place. They included:

- SPOT awards were given to people demonstrating the desired behaviors at any time.
- In addition to the bonus already in place, $1 million was put aside to reinforce PRIDE values.
- For the first time, every location started to send leaders to HQ for meetings with top leaders to hand out awards.
- DBS Cares was developed to focus on the right benefits. It included rewards, recognition and mobility.
- An initiative to fill new positions internally was begun. For example, when a leader in Hong Kong resigned, it resulted in six people changing positions across businesses and borders.
- DBS Academy was established. As part of the Academy, leaders identify the skills and training required to successfully implement the strategy. Training content, written by employees of the bank, is offered at three levels: Foundation, Advanced and Mastery. Some courses are compulsory and some are optional. As a result, the bank has 250 training roadmaps for employees featuring 10% classroom training, 70% learning on the job and 20% mentoring.

- Every year the highly coveted Banking the Asian Way Awards are presented by bank leaders to teams and individuals who exhibit the desired values. The awards help deliver this key message: "The bank will take a risk on you, but you must take a risk on yourself," as stated by Lee Yan Hong, Managing Director and Head of Group Human Resources.

While implementing the performance management system, leaders also successfully integrated reviews into the way the bank operates. Today, reviews are conducted at these intervals:

- Weekly Executive Committee (Exco) Meetings—to ensure corporate governance around the implementation
- Group Management Committee (GMC) Reviews—to meet with Piyush every two weeks and include visits to countries and clients
- Mid-Month Reviews (MMR)—to discuss the business pipeline, credit position and current financials. They are held every month.
- Scorecard Review—to assess strategy. They are held every six months between Piyush and each of the MC members.
- CEO Business/Support units and Country reviews to course correct if necessary. They are conducted between Piyush and the Business/Support Unit country heads bi-quarterly.
- Employee Reviews—to have performance conversations ranging from goal setting to mid- and end-year reviews. These reviews are held three times a year.

"Business review meetings take place monthly. We have standardized infrastructure across countries facilitated by common IT platforms. We measure the performance of business units not just by P&L but by KPIs that are relevant to the business."
—Chng Sok Hui, Chief Financial Officer

DBS Wealth Management Success Story

The success of the implementation of the DBS House is reflected in the growth of the bank's Wealth Management business.

For example, Tan Su Shan joined DBS in 2010 as head of Private Banking and Asset Management. She identified that the bank had prospective Wealth Management clients who were the "silent affluent"—that is, they were bank customers doing various wealth management activities with other banks. They considered DBS a safe bank to use for, as an example, deposits. When there was turbulence in the market, though, they weren't queuing to get their money out. Instead, they were putting their money in.

Su Shan's goal became winning their confidence so they would increase the bank's share of both wallet and market. As part of the new strategy, Su Shan and her team developed the wealth continuum in 2010. They designed it to ensure the right value proposition for each customer segment, combined with the right operating model.

Private Banking refers to having more than $5 million in the account; a Treasures Private Client has between $1.5 and $5 million; a Treasures Client has less than $1.5 million and more than $350,000. This wealth continuum not only represents a journey for the client but also for employees, offering them career progression as they move from Treasures to Treasures Private Client to Private Banking.

Su Shan realized she had to work with the consumer side of the bank to integrate the wealth continuum. This resulted in her taking the highly extraordinary step of asking Piyush to demote her so she would report to the Consumer Banking head. Why? Because that's where the customers she wanted to target for Wealth Management were already doing business. The idea was to move clients and staff members along the wealth continuum.

An issue arose about taking the best clients and employees from each segment and progressing them, but it was still encouraged. This was a way to develop and respect both the clients and the employees.

To inspire her Wealth Management development team, Su Shan explained in her regular town hall meetings that the bank had all the necessary parts of running that bank as smoothly as a Ferrari. People just had to pull the parts together and believe they could compete with anyone. Today, customers compliment the bank on working seamlessly as one bank.

In addition, employees were trained to know what was needed to deal in capital markets. The front-line staff had to take the CMFAS exam—a specific exam for financial markets—and everyone passed! Today, most of those who pioneered in the wealth management area in 2010 remain with the bank today.

As the people and the technology improved, significant changes were made to how products were sold. Relationship Managers (RM) were empowered to sell "open," which meant they not only offered bank products but counselled clients on what services were best for them. Technology enabled the right products to be sold to the right customer. For example, if a RM tried to sell a high-risk product to a person with a low-risk profile, the system would not allow it.

As the Wealth Management business built momentum and evolved along the wealth continuum, Shu Shan looked toward what was next: Digital 2.0 and leveraging the latest technology. She and her team presented their plans to Piyush. At the start of the meeting, Shu Shan's eBusiness head started the presentation to Piyush and the CEO walked out! Why? After the shock, Su Shan realized she had to fully embrace Digital 2.0 and could not delegate it. This was the message Piyush was sending. She embraced the challenge.

Early on when implementing Digital 2.0, Su Shan realized they were looking at the journey from inside out, not outside in—that is, designing from the bank's perspective and not the customers'.

She made sure Digital 2.0 focused on making banking safe, simple, relevant and speedy for customers. Today, electronic banking is designed around what they want (not what the banks want them to know). They also made sure it was easy to call for assistance if required.

In addition, to incorporate more mobile opportunities, they switched the name from e-wealth to i-wealth to reflect the shift toward mobile—with great success. Over time, the number of digital logins has exceeded the number of branch walk-ins.

This Wealth Management success exemplifies the overall implementation of the DBS House.

Chapter Seventeen

DBS Bank Today

Customers now say that DBS is a different bank than it was 10 years ago. Once at the bottom of the Customer Satisfaction Index of Singapore (CSISG),[111] DBS Bank tops the list today. Gallup ranks it as one of the top 5% in employee engagement globally. Aon Hewitt[112] ranks it as one of the top 25 companies for leaders in the world. DBS also ranks as the number one brand in Singapore and SE Asia—even ahead of Singapore Airlines.

Just as important, employees feel proud to work at DBS. They love being in this fun environment and doing their jobs. They acknowledge that the rigor to completely follow through on this implementation journey was a huge achievement within the bank.

Reflecting on the bank's journey, Piyush said there was nothing major he and his leaders would have done differently. However, one area where they would have liked to do more is growth in the big geographies—China, India and Indonesia.

---

111 CSISG is a landmark measure of customer satisfaction cutting across sectors and sub-sectors in the services industry of Singapore.

112 http://www.aon.com/human-capital-consulting/thought-leadership/leadership/aon-hewitt-top-companies-for-leaders-winners.jsp#1

While the large corporate franchise has done well, the SME and consumer businesses have been challenged by distribution limitations due to regulations resulting in longer payback periods. The bank is focused on harnessing the digital opportunity as a game changer to extend its reach into the larger geographies.

The leaders could also have brought people on board more quickly, but they were diverted got distracted in the middle of the implementation by an opportunity to acquire Indonesia's Bank Danamon. Unfortunately, the proposed transaction was in stalemate languished for over a year as they waited for approval from Indonesia's financial regulators. Eventually, the bank's leaders walked away.

"The way people live is changing dramatically."
—Piyush

The New Strategy: Digital and Customer Journey Evolves as One

According to Piyush, digital changes should have started in the banking industry sooner than any other industry because it deals in data and information as opposed to physical goods. It's not that banks need to move to the digital world; rather, the digital world is moving to banks and that requires a different strategy.

Specifically, banks have to compete with organizations from outside banking that are much better at digitizing services. The new competitive landscape comprises of fintechs (an emerging financial services sector that combines finances and technology) that are unraveling the financial services value chain. It's not only about making cosmetic changes to websites or apps; the digital world is where people are engaging and doing business. As an example, by 2014, the number of DBS customers using internet and mobile banking platforms increased to more than 2.7 million and 1 million respectively. Today, internet and mobile transactions average more than 24 million each month.

Piyush stated that in the next five years, every part of the banking industry will experience a disruption at every critical point of the value chain, treasury, FX payments. Therefore, the bank aims to digitalize the customer journey and help its employees adopt a digital mindset. This involves an end-to-end view of customer experience. The interaction begins *before* they come into the bank, which requires everyone to think about the real job the customer wants done and how it can be fulfilled. DBS is deepening its journey thinking with more 1,500 staff trained and over a hundred customer journeys conducted in 2015. This is an outside-in view to banking; employees think of how to fulfil their jobs in a way that is invisible and effortless as they engage with customers' needs in their world. From there, they can embed changes.

To Piyush and DBS, the holy grail for the bank is to make banking "invisible"—that is, to make banking so seamlessly integrated into customers' lives that they don't see themselves as performing a financial transaction. This will require DBS to be flexible and nimble while having a relentless customer focus. To leverage digital capabilities and make the customer experience painless requires marrying the strengths of a traditional bank and a technology company.

Also as part of the new strategy, the bank aims to be the first-to-last banking service for its customers. This means being a customer's first account opening, loan, mortgage, salary, IPO, and more while keeping that relationship through the generations.

The dimensions of this digital strategy involve tweaking these priorities:

1. Create a positive customer experience through interface that streamlines the whole journey. For example, the bank introduced an app called "PayLah" (digital wallet), which allows banking at your fingertips. It's designed for convenience and security but also social fun. Another example would be having digital channels to on-board customers for scale. DBS launched Online Account Opening for customers in which SMEs can be on-boarded in a simple, fast and easy process online. DBS was the first bank in Asia to digitize its loan application. In Singapore, SMEs can apply for up to 11 types of loan products online. They can track the application online and receive instant notifications on the loan processing. SME customers in Hong Kong are also able to apply for loans via a mobile app and receive in-principle approval within an hour.

2. Digitalize services through mobile means and analytics while eliminating paper. More than a front-end effort, it has to be embraced throughout the bank. DBS has made efforts to completely digitize bank transactions

such as using SOA (Service-Oriented Architecture) and an API (Application Programme Interface) framework to eliminate paper and provide instant fulfilment. Customers are beginning to see income and expense benefits from this. But this journey is constantly moving toward a technology architecture based on micro-services.

3. Create a new business model based on leveraging technology. This means shifting away from revenue that's earned from fees and margins.
4. For employees, nurture a sense of purpose in the work environment that will act as a compass for making decisions and creating an empowered, engaged workforce.

Part of the journey aims to provide the path of least resistance for customers conducting banking transactions. The bank will be awarded business in a variety of categories as a result. A recent example is the app Home Connect. Banks usually focus on providing mortgage loans, but customers basically want to find a home they can afford. The app engages the customer from the very first step—property search and fact finding. Linking up the Urban Redevelopment Authority of Singapore, the app is wired into the database of every single house in Singapore. During the house-hunting process, customers can take their phones, go to any house in Singapore and scan the house in augmented reality. The app provides information such as the last transacted price, rentals and the nearest amenities. The app also contains a loan calculator to help customers work out the financing needed, and they can also contact a DBS loan specialist via the app.

By engaging our customers at an early stage in that journey, DBS can make an impression that leads to business outcomes.

> **"Growing your business is our business."**
> **—Chu Chong Lim, Head of SME Banking**

Innovation and a Digital Mindset

In 2014, the bank started doing hackathons to assist in creating a digital mindset as well generate ideas. Teaching top performing employees to be innovative and adopt their mindset has changed their perceptions. Today, they spend time on solving problems in the bank one day a month by taking on a problem, a prototype and even a product. Their innovation comes from holding diverse conversations not only among people in the bank but with other parties.

Through participation in various bank programs such as accelerators, employees gain tremendous value working with start-ups. DBS's employees are able to broaden their thinking. Start-up companies in turn benefit from their banking expertise, the capital they bring by connecting them with the private bank and corporate clients as well as the network DBS creates with other eco-system partners. Together, DBS and its partners commercialize many of the ideas generated while giving their employees the tools to re-imagine how banking services can be delivered to customers.

To promote innovation, the bank has introduced a crowd-sourcing platform to support (or not) new ideas. Ideas from employees are shared online and colleagues vote for them, with prizes being awarded to those who came up with the winning ideas.

Employees are also using external data as well as bank data and even creating data that didn't used to exist. For example, they are placing sensors in ATMs to track and predict, through algorithms, when the ATMs will break down. In this way and more, the bank is watching, observing and learning from its customers.

Bank leaders have also introduced the Digital Index to measure how well a digital mindset has become embedded in the DBS culture, thus determining how successful their digital initiatives have been.

Making Banking Joyful

Five years ago, implementing the DBS House was predominantly a top-down process in the bank. Today, it's bubbling up from the ground level. For Piyush, he used to conduct reviews to check that things were done. Today, he hears about 80% of the activities for the first time.

There is a shift across the bank to make banking a joyful, not dull, experience for customers. It involves creating a sense of happiness when dealing with the bank as well as peace of mind and enjoyable interactions. Speaking directly to the bank's value and intent, it also means being part of customers' happy occasions such as births and marriages.

After endorsing the digital mindset, strategy implementation is considered easy to do because of the hard work completed to date. The bank has established a culture of continuous improvement. For example, 29 best practices have been set on how to run a project such as ensuring sponsorship by bringing in stakeholders before a project starts, then conducting tests, having key measures, training and more. The bank's Last Mile program runs at the end of every project to make sure results are obtained. Those involved ask, "Was the project's solution Useful, Usable and Used?"

DBS Bank's reputation externally and its people's confidence internally have dramatically improved. Within four years of starting its implementation, it's become known as the best bank in Asia. Much of the credit goes to its leaders and the strong partnership and support from board members.

World's Best Digital Bank Award

In 2016, DBS Bank became the first bank to be named World's Best Digital Bank at the prestigious *Euromoney* Awards for Excellence. According to the *Euromoney* magazine, "The award for the world's best digital bank was one of the hardest fought of all, with BBVA, Citi and ING named as other strong contenders for this hotly contested award. In the end, DBS pipped the others for the global award because of the all-pervasive nature of its digital transformation."

DBS's win marks the first time a Singaporean and Asian bank has won a global accolade from *Euromoney*, one of the world's leading financial publications. *Euromoney* also named DBS Asia's Best Bank, another first for a Singapore bank.

Today, DBS Bank is primed to become the best in the world!

Chapter Eighteen

Uncommon Practices from Excellence in Execution Organizations

This chapter summarizes and reinforces the most essential *uncommon practices* described throughout the book and is also a keynote I deliver. Visit www.bridgesconsultancy.com/keynotes/nine-uncommon-practices-new-business-landscape-keynote for more information.

1. 90 Day Chunks (Chapter Seven)

Challenge:

In some organizations, actions are set to be completed in many months and are often not completed or even started. People put off working on the action because they think they still have plenty of time or because it's a large action, or they are not inspired to act and they just can't get started.

Solution:

Set actions that are achievable in 90-day compartments. This makes the pressure to start working on the action more timely, the action more manageable and the impact more immediate. As a result, people take the right actions and the execution builds traction. You then quickly see early wins that can be shared across the organization. Theory promises and success sells. The successes encourage people to participate and also demonstrate the strategy in action. If you need more than 90 days to complete any action, divide it into small segments.

2. Execution Planning is Part of Your Strategy Planning (Chaper Two)

Challenge:

Organizations often roll out the new strategy without having a comprehensive execution plan. After the initial fanfare, the excitement and interest dissipate, and it's back to BAU (Business As Usual).

Solution:

Plan your execution in detail as part of your strategy, for a good strategy is one that is executed well.

3. Structure Success (Chapter Five)

Challenge:

After crafting the strategy, leaders return to their offices often without a framework to guide them through their implementation journey. This leaves them unsure where to start. It can result in executing the strategy differently across each business and even duplicating work.

Solution:

Unlike crafting strategy, only a handful of tools and techniques are available for executing it. A framework guides the whole organization through the implementation journey, ensuring right actions are taken everywhere. I recommend using the Implementation Compass™.[113] Other popular frameworks are the Execution Premium[114] from Kaplan and Norton and Kotter International's 8-Step Process for Leading Change.[115]

---

113 http://www.implementation-hub.com/implementation_framework
114 http://thepalladiumgroup.com/knowledge/Palladium-Execution-Premium-Process-XPP
115 http://www.kotterinternational.com/the-8-step-process-for-leading-change/

4. Choice is King (Chapter Eight)

Challenge:

Only one person in five—the Maverick—feels positive about adopting a new strategy. People in general don't like to be told what to do as much as choose actions themselves.

Solution:

People commit more easily to taking the right actions when they are empowered rather than instructed. They are more committed to outcomes they set themselves by a ratio of almost five to one. Today, they are more self-directed than ever and prefer to choose their own work.

5. Explain the Why before the How (Chapter Seven)

Challenge:

Organizations charge into the execution without explaining why the transformation is needed. People are pulled along reluctantly and resent taking new actions when they see no reason to change.

Solution:

People need to understand the emotional and logical reasons for the transformation. They also like to be teased into the changes required. The philosophy is to not tell the whole story but reveal only parts of it and let people come to their own conclusions on why the organization must transform. This results in higher levels of engagement.

6. Keep Communicating the Right Messages (Chapter Seven)

Challenge:

If the communication about the strategy dissipates, as it frequently does, then people's interest in the execution also dissolves. They focus on what's being discussed and measured. When leaders stop talking about the strategy execution, people stop working on it. Many leaders know this but still don't do it. It is the number one reason why execution fails.

Solution:

Nurture your communication throughout the implementation journey. It could be sharing progress against the objectives, problems, customer feedback, best practices, lessons learned, milestones achieved, strategy deviations and/or uncommon practices. Keep communicating the right messages

7. Less is More (Chapter Seven)

Challenge:

When people have too much to do, frequently nothing gets done. They become lost in the complexity and retreat from participating in the execution.

Solution:

It is better to focus on fewer objectives than more, so ask your people to do less while still allowing them to have a choice. This frees up people's time to act on what is important and allows the allocation of resources to support them in succeeding.

8. Abandon Yesterday (Chapter Ten)

Challenge:

The pace of work is accelerating and you can no longer expect yesterday's performance to deliver tomorrow's results. Strategies are lasting for shorter times than ever and we are living in a time of disruption.

Solution:

Don't rely on yesterday's success for tomorrow's growth. Develop an agile culture and encourage people to be self-directed. Then constantly review your strategic landscape for BMD (Business Model Disruption) and track your execution performance.

9. Check Ins (Chapter Fourteen)

Challenge:

With the pace of work today, many organizations can no longer wait 12 months to review and reinforce the actions of employees. They need more frequent reinforcement.

Solution:

Consider abolishing annual appraisals. Instead, meet with your people every 90 days to reinforce the right actions. These focus more on future performance than reviewing past performance and inspire people to keep doing the right actions.

10. Point Out What's Right (Chapter Fourteen)

Challenge:

No one knows the exact path of the implementation journey. We start moving and along the way, people try different things. Some work and some don't. Far too often leaders only point out what is wrong.

Solution:

Be conscious of balancing *what can be improved* with *what people are doing right*. It's just as important to praise people for taking the right actions as it is to coach them through the wrong actions.

11. Review Rhythm (Chapter Fourteen)

Challenge:

In some organizations, the strategy execution is only reviewed once or twice a year. Leaders become distracted by other activities and take their attention away from the execution. When they do this, so will their people, allowing small issues to snowball into large problems.

Solution:

People need to be constantly reviewed on how they are doing. Similarly, leaders need to regularly check on the progress by instilling a *Review Rhythm* into the culture. That means every week, fortnight, quarter and year, people are reviewed on their execution actions.

12. Make It Your Own (Part Two)

Challenge:

Because each organization is unique, you have to identify what will work and what won't for *your* culture. Concepts, ideas and frameworks can be adopted, but they must be translated into your way of doing things.

Solution:

Customize your execution by understanding the idiosyncrasies of the organization. Invest in the time to understand your organization's culture and the impact it has on driving your execution.

13. Implementation Never Goes According to Plan (Chapter Four)

Challenge:

After all the hard planning and preparation, as soon as you start to execute, circumstances change—one of the few absolute truths in business. Also, there are no guaranteed right answers, and there are different stress points for each organization.

Solution:

Your Excellence in Execution approach must be agile and susceptible to the changes. So must your role as a leader. Constantly check not only what is happening inside the organization but also what outside influencers are present.

Please email your favorite uncommon practice to robin@bridgesconsultancy.com and enjoy your implementation journey.

APPENDICES
AND RESOURCES

Appendix A

Summary of Toolkits and Checklists

Page	Toolkits
19	What is the Philosophy in *Your* Organization?
28	Alignment Exercise
55	SanderMan's Cloud Solution
62	Strategic Priorities Exercise
73	The Decoy Effect
74	Out for Lunch
74	Priming People
97	Six Common Pitfalls in Creating Awareness
101	Nine Tactics for Moving People Over the Wall
107	Nine Steps for Writing Down the Reasons to Transform
110	Combine Logic and Emotion in Your Communications
111	3X3 Rule + 7X7 Rule
115	Communication Foundation Workshop
128	Creating a Mavericks Network
147	The Impact of Culture in Your Organization
149	Creating a Culture of Excellence (CoEx)
181	Questions Defining Areas to Excel
182	How will we transform the way people work

Page	Checklists
24	Leading with Authenticity and Sincerity
25	Ways to Carve Out Time and Energy to Transform the Business
57	Strategy Execution Office Responsibilities
59	The Role of a Middle Manager
76	Six Steps for Creating a Culture of Accountability
113	Second Wave of Communication
119	Inspiring Your People
169	The Vital Few Guiding Questions
170	15 Best Practices for Using Measures to Manage the Business
186	Eliminating or Exiting Current Business
216	Self-Directed People
227	Benefits of Structured Reviews

Language of Excellence in Execution

Language	Explanation
Baseline	Current measured performance
BMD	Business Model Disruption
BSC	Balanced Scorecard
CEM	Career Ending Move
CoEx	Culture of Excellence
Communication Foundation Workshop	One-day workshop to identify an organization's communication goals and initiate branding
Create Awareness	Inform and inspire people about the strategy, creating a sense of urgency and explaining why they are part of the transformation
Critical Processes	Where the organization must excel to deliver the strategy
CSF	Critical Success Factors
Execution Juxtaposition	A literary term referring to two or more ideas and/or actions placed side by side
First Wave Communications	Creating the communication plan and launch of the strategy to Create Awareness of the strategy execution
Follow Through	Regularly reinforcing and reviewing performance
HOW	How Organizations Win
Legacy Actions	Old actions that were successful in executing the old strategy

Create a "To-Stop" List	Empowering employees to identify and eliminate work that has become obsolete or isn't adding value to the new way of working
Over the Wall	The rationale people need at the start of the journey to understand why they should adopt the new strategy
PMI	What is the strategy Positioning? What is your Message? What Image represents the Message?
Readiness2Execute Assessment	Assess your execution capabilities before launching the new strategy
Review Rhythm	A pattern and expectation that progress is being checked at regular intervals and then acted on
Second Wave Communications	Ensures nurturing the communication by sharing the right messages and information repeatedly over time to Build Excellence and Follow Through
Strategic Inflection Point	Something that causes leaders to make a fundamental change in business strategy
Strategic Objectives	The critical, must-achieve, make-or-break organizational performance outcomes
Strategy Cadence	The rate at which the execution is revolving
Strategic Inflection Point	Transition to a new way of operating
Strategy Map	One-page document that translates the strategy into objectives and how the two elements interact
Strategy Scorecard	Measures of the strategy objectives that drive the right actions
Three Broad Themes of Execution	Create Awareness, Build Excellence and Follow Through
Vital Few	The essential measures to track the execution of the strategy
WEX-FM	What's Expected From Me
WII-FM	What's In It For Me

Appendix C

DBS PRIDE Values, Performance and Key Awards

We believe that here in DBS, people truly are our biggest asset. While modern technology has helped to transform the banking sector, we are ultimately still a people-driven business. As we continue to expand, our goal is to embed a set of firm values into the organization so that we will develop a distinctive DBS performance culture with PRIDE! We want our people in DBS to be known for their commitment, innovation and sense of empowerment.

At the heart of all that we do, we want our people in DBS to be see beyond the day-to-day and to be guided by our values. In short, we want our people to take pride in the way we conduct business and behave as engaged corporate citizens.

Purpose-driven

We Create Impact Beyond Banking

At DBS, we believe the impact we create goes beyond banking . . . because what we do touches real people, real businesses and real lives. We strive to be a long-term Asian partner, committed to making banking joyful and trustworthy and transforming Asia for the better.

Relationship-led
We Collaborate to Win For DBS

At DBS, we build long-lasting relationships and strong teams. We collaborate by working together to find better solutions. We treat each other and our partners with respect.

Innovative
We Embrace Change to Add Value

At DBS, we embrace change and we are not afraid to do things differently. We are encouraged to challenge the status quo and find innovative ways to serve our customers well and create delightful experiences.

Decisive
We Think, Act, Own

At DBS, ours is a workplace where people walk in confidence knowing that it's not about who you are, or where you come from... but about what you can do. People thrive here as they are given the freedom to decide, take ownership and make things happen.

E!
We Are Everything Fun!

At DBS, people are excited and energized about being part of a great team. We have fun and celebrate together!

Performance

Number of employees: 21 000 persons.

Sales per Businesses

	2013		2014		
	SGD *(in Million)*	%	SGD *(in Million)*	%	**Delta**
Institutional Banking	4,676		4,967		+5.86%
Consumer Banking/Wealth Management	2,538		2,882		+11.94%
Treasury	1,034		1,102		+6.17%
Others	679		667		
Goodwill and Intangibles	-	-	-	-	-

Sales per Regions

	2013		2014		
	SGD *(in Million)*	%	SGD *(in Million)*	%	Delta
Singapore	5,415		5,950		+9.14%
Hong Kong	1,863		1,900		+1.95%
Rest of Greater China	743.00		950.00		+21.79%
South and Southeast Asia	600.00		552.00		-8.7%
Rest of the World	306.00		266.00		-15.04%

Source: http://www.4-traders.com/DBS-GROUP-HOLDINGS-LTD-6491408/company/

[Source: DBS Investor Relations website > Performance Summaries]

Key Awards (up to Dec 2015)

DBS has been winning regional awards in the past few years, which validates its strategic intent of being the Asian Bank of Choice for the New Asia.

In 2012, DBS was recognized for its leadership in the region, having been named "Asia's Best Bank" by *The Banker*, a member publication of the Financial Times group.

In 2014, DBS was named "Best Bank in Asia-Pacific" by *Global Finance*, a New York-based magazine. This marked the first time an Asian bank has won this prestigious award since the award's inception more than two decades ago.

In 2015, DBS Bank was named "Safest Bank in Asia" for the seventh consecutive year, also by Global Finance. In addition, DBS was named as the "Asian Bank of the Year" by IFR Asia, the first Singapore Bank to win this award. To top off the accolades for 2015, DBS was recognized as the "Best Asia Commercial Bank" by *FinanceAsia*, a leading Asian financial publication.

The bank has also begun to win global awards as it pursues world-class excellence while maintaining its regional focus. It has been named the "Best Transaction Bank" and the "Most Innovative Private Bank" globally by *The Banker* and *Global Finance* respectively. This is a testament to the bank's relentless focus on customer service and leveraging innovation to deliver a world-class customer experience.

The focus on cultural change and people development at DBS is also bearing fruit. The bank has been recognized as one of the world's top 25 companies (ranked 18th) for leaders by Aon Hewitt. The bank has also been awarded the Gallup Great Workplace Award for three consecutive years.

Asia's best

Making a mark globally

Bridges Business Consultancy Int

Bridges Business Consultancy Int is a specialist in strategy implementation. Bridges was founded at the start of the millennium to research, develop and integrate corporate strategy execution. *This is our singular focus.* We know from our work and research that more organizations fail than succeed at strategy implementation. Our goal is to reverse this staggering failure rate.

We work with governments, multinational organizations and local businesses in five continents to assist their leaders in executing strategy successfully. Our pioneering activities include:

- **Implementation Compass**™—a framework for strategy execution
- One of the world's first **blogs** and **smartphone apps** on the subject
- The world's first portal, the **Implementation Hub**—with over 500 resources
- **Five books** published on the subject
- **Readiness2Execute assessment** of your execution capabilities

269

Strategy implementation is not rocket science; it is common sense. But just because it is common sense does *not* mean it is common practice. We are here to share what works and what to avoid. At heart, we are a team who truly believes in—and passionately focuses on—successfully implementing strategy.

For more information on Bridges visit www.bridgesconsultancy.com

Bridges Products and Offerings

'Masterclass'

HOW to Achieve Excellence in Execution

Leverage the mindset, toolset and skillset from successful
organizations and learn the secrets of execution

This exceptionally engaging three-day interactive Masterclass is based on this book. It's best suited for leaders embarking on strategy execution and those already underway who need support. Not for the faint hearted, it delves into what it takes to achieve Excellence in Execution—and that means doing things differently.

In this Masterclass, you learn up-to-date approaches, thinking, language, frameworks, secrets and uncommon practices as well as tools and techniques. During the sessions, you start to build your company's execution plan and discuss the key content required to achieve Excellence in Execution. Content includes Strategy Cadence, Three Broad Theme of Execution, Culture of Accountability, Aligning Projects and Review Rhythm. You discuss in-depth case studies, organizational challenges and videos based on neuroscience.

All participants receive a soft copy of the material, a framework for implementing their organization's strategy, Robin's book on implementation and one-year free access to the world's only strategy implementation portal, The Implementation Hub.

For more information visit www.bridgesconsultancy.com/bridges-courses/masterclass-how-to-achieve-excellence-in-execution

Implementation Hub
Your Portal to Strategy Implementation Success

The Implementation Hub is the first portal in the world dedicated to strategy implementation. This exciting, informative and stimulating site serves those who want access to implementation resources in the most effective and efficient way. You can easily find what you are looking for in one place rather than searching online endlessly.

It's central depository is loaded with more than 510 videos, templates, techniques, tips, best practices, media presentations, case studies, audits, tools and other useful resources. They all support you in either understanding more about strategy implementation or providing you with materials and skills you require for success.

The four broad categories on the Hub are:

1. *Introduction to strategy implementation*—why implementation has become a leadership field in its own right and a competitive differentiator
2. *A framework*—the Implementation Compass™ identifies the eight areas of excellence for execution
3. *Tools, Tips & Techniques*—to support you throughout your journey
4. *Resources*—additional materials you may require

Each area has multiple sections within it. The portal's site map provides an overview of the HUB and the search function allows you to look for specific topics. New content is added every two weeks.

The most popular section is "One Minute on Implementation". This has leaders and academics sharing a key message in 60 seconds.

For more information visit www.implementation-hub.com

A Toolkit and Structured Approach to Implementing Actions within 90 Days

IMPACT is a toolkit with a structured approach for implementing actions within 90 days. It includes templates, guides and tools to ensure a successful implementation. IMPACT starts after you have created the plan of action as your meeting or workshop is ending. In theory, your plan of action is a fait accompli. In practice, it's a different story. Upon returning to the organization and despite team members' best intentions, most action plans are not executed.

Most of us start with the right intentions but somewhere between thought and action, we lose focus, we lose direction, we lose commitment. IMPACT bridges this gap.

Its design overcomes the most frequent challenges and guides the team to success through its structured approach. Practical and easy to use, it adopts best practices from around the world. At the heart of it is six Action Team Meetings (ATMs) held every two weeks to make sure team members are doing what they said they would do.

You receive a customized bag that includes: Team Mentor's, Leader's and Member's Guide; IMPACT Posters; Certificate; Wobblers; IMPACT Pens; USB Flash Disk containing templates and soft copies and other materials.

IMPACT Kit is reusable and is just US$500 which includes packing and shipping.

To order, visit www.bridgesconsultancy.com/shop
or email www.bridgesconsultancy.com

E-Pocket Book of
Excellence in Execution
136 Key Messages for Your Success

 Leaders in organizations are frequently called on to execute a new strategy. But their training has been in *planning* strategies, not *executing* them. This has left a gap in the skills and knowledge required for achieving Excellence in Execution.

What happens? People repeat the mistakes made in previous executions and get poor results—again. Based on research since 2000, two-thirds of executions fail and leaders habitually underestimate the whole execution challenge.

Many leaders struggle to find the knowledge they need to do things differently—especially in a form that's succinct and easy to use. Only a few books address this subject and fewer yet highlight the core messages that are critical to success.

The Pocket Book of Excellence in Execution: 136 Key Messages for Your Success fills this gap with a concise collection of essential lessons. Its messages are organized under the eight areas for Excellence in Execution. These practical tips guide you in overcoming key challenges, with each one featuring a nugget for implementing strategy. You would apply these bite-size tips along the implementation journey as you put your new strategy in place.

You can order this book at www.bridgesconsultancy.com/product-category/ books or at www.amazon.com/Pocket-Book-Excellence-Execution-Messages-ebook/dp/B00K5J8AV2/ref=cm_cr_pr_pb_t

Beyond Strategy
The Leader's Role in Successful Implementation

International Bestseller

Due to the staggering failure of organizations to deliver on strategy promises, implementation has become an integral part of strategy discussions. In *Beyond Strategy*, Robin Speculand shifts the emphasis from *why strategy implementation is important* (the focus of his international bestseller *Bricks to Bridges*) to *what leaders must do differently*. When something needs to change, that change starts with the leaders.

Strategy implementation can't simply be delegated; leaders must take charge. *Beyond Strategy* provides the model, structure and specific actions for leaders at all levels to go beyond strategy and deliver on their promises.

Beyond Strategy is divided into the eight areas of the Implementation Compass™—a tool that identifies the eight global best practices of strategy implementation. Each chapter summarizes the actions leaders must take in the eight areas. You'll find this must-have book succinct, action orientated, and packed with practical tips and case studies. It provides a breakthrough in understanding strategy implementation itself *and* explains a leader's responsibility to execute it well.

To order *Beyond Strategy*, go to www.bridgesconsultancy.com/shop or www.amazon.com/Beyond-Strategy-Leaders-Successful-Implementation/dp/0470824980.

Bricks to Bridges
Make Your Strategy Come Alive

International
Bestseller

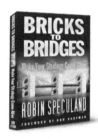

How refreshing! A comprehensive way for leaders in any kind of organization to make desired changes "stick."

Because of its graphically fun presentation and thorough approach that spells out what to do, *Bricks to Bridges* has a way of making change seem easy. Author Robin Speculand, an expert consultant and facilitator on strategy implementation, brings his experience and solid methodology to the printed page.

No excuses anymore! If you follow the Implementation Compass™—a tool he created that guides the process from start to finish—you'll see the genius in Speculand's method.

Why is an Implementation Compass even needed in the first place? Because most of the energy required initiating implementation goes into designing a new strategy. Yet that effort gets wasted because the strategy is never implemented properly—a frequent occurrence.

Speculand's style is blunt, clear and didactic. He takes no shortcuts in explaining how leaders can successfully implement the strategies they've created… from their launch to their review cycles to their redefinitions.

More than that, Speculand makes sure the key players implementing any strategy—the employees—are in the center of the action. They're the people who bring great ideas down to earth. This aspect makes *Brick to Bridges* especially practical and powerful. It addresses how to communicate what you want with staff members, reinforced by how to reward and recognize them for achieving the desired outcomes. If you apply the author's suggestions on how to deal with different personalities, you'll keep everyone engaged at every stage of the implementation journey.

To order *Bricks to Bridges,* go to www.bridgesconsultancy.com/shop.

Turning It On
Surefire Business Stories to
Ignite, Excite and Entertain

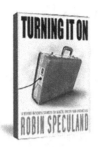

What does a magic stone from India have to do with communication? What does Thomas Edison's philosophy say about the way you run your business? What do penguins shivering in Antarctica have to do with teamwork?

If you want a new way to arouse your team, captivate an audience or punch up your next presentation, *Turning It On* is the resource for you! Packed with incredible and truly engaging tales, Robin Speculand offers creative ways to add substance and sparkle to all your communications. Read *Turning It On* and turn on the creativity in your meetings, presentations and newsletters. This is one reference book that will *not* gather dust on your shelf!

To order *Turning It On,* go to www.bridgesconsultancy.com/product-category/books.

Implementation Cards

Want to make a difference fast? Pick up a set of Implementation Cards for your organization. These novel, effective and powerful cards allow you to identify the Critical Success Factors for implementing your organization's strategy.

Learn from previous mistakes made in your own organization and others, and then turn them around to your advantage. Each set (designed for six to eight players) comes with instructions on how to create an interactive and highly engaging 45-minute session. As a result, you can identify the Critical Success Factors for any project, innovation or strategy.

This fun, practical, easy-to-use tool will smooth your way to a highly successful implementation.

Details at www.bridgesconsultancy.com/shop.

Building Your Execution Plan
182 Strategy Implementation Questions

Leaders have been struggling with the challenge of executing strategy for too long. With more strategy executions failing than succeeding, a different attitude and approach is required.

Building Your Execution Plan directly addresses this issue and supports leadership teams to develop a comprehensive execution plan as part of an organization's strategy planning.

The execution can't be an afterthought when crafting your strategy; it must be part of the whole planning process. It is both an eBook and printed book.

You'll find 182 questions about implementing your strategy designed to provoke your thinking and ensure you address all of the required areas to achieve excellence in execution. They have been extracted from this book.

The 182 questions are divided into the Three Broad Themes required to achieve excellence in execution: 1) Create Awareness, 2) Build Excellence and 3) Follow Through. They have been developed from the research conducted since 2000 by my consulting company, Bridges Business Consultancy Int, and from our work with clients to develop their execution plans and implement their strategies.

As reflected by the high failure rate, executing strategy is not easy. But when you succeed, you'll have a tremendous payoff. *Building Your Execution Plan* enables you to deliver your strategy promises to your stakeholders on your implementation journey.

You can order this book at www.bridgesconsultancy.com/product-category/books

Acknowledgments

Of all of my books, this one has taken the longest to research and write to meet my aim of providing you with the HOW for your organization to execute its strategy. In fact, it has taken longer than all my other manuscripts combined. Along the way, various people have assisted me to keep refining it and to achieve my goal.

I would like to first thank my partner Gracekelly for her patience and support. I locked myself away for months at a time to write, and then I bombarded her with ideas and questions on the best way to frame the material.

My editor Barbara McNichol has worked with me for more than 11 years. She is not only an amazing editor and highly supportive but also knows the topic of execution so well now, she contributes to content as well as editing.

A special thank you goes to DBS Bank and its CEO Piyush Gupta for allowing me access to capture their execution story. Sandy Tan, Diane Seethor and Alvin Ee Aing Tan were particularly patient in arranging interviews, answering questions and reviewing material.

I am fortunate to have a network of friends who have injected improvements into the content along the 30 months it has taken to write and publish this book. In particular, I would like to thank Michel Sznajer, a patient and supportive friend. He read the early drafts of all my books and provided valuable input while demonstrating that less said is more. Thank you to Laura Gordon and Gary Berman for the constant support and friendship since our childhood. Bruce Scheer has been a colleague and good friend whom I meet in various corners of the world to discuss concepts. Bala G., also a friend since I moved to Singapore, has provided feedback for all my books as well as stimulating lunch conversations.

I thank Professor Michael Netzley (SMU), Sandeep Sander, Vaughn Richtor, Dr. Scott J. Simmerman and Professor Serguei Netessine (INSEAD) for taking time to share their views on executing strategy and reading my manuscript. I also thank Reuben Khafi for keeping me sane through the writing, my friend Andrew Lim for the company in the morning during his classical radio show in Singapore and my mentor, Ron Kaufman, for the constant wisdom and guidance.

Selecting a publisher in not an easy challenge, and I thank the team at Morgan James for working with me to produce the book we wanted.

The excellent designs in the book have been created by Jeramine Erize, whom I also sincerely thank.

Finally, a special thank you to my father who has supported and encouraged me all of my life. Most recently, he showed fortitude and provided invaluable feedback as I worked on this book.

Morgan James
Speakers Group

↗ www.TheMorganJamesSpeakersGroup.com

We connect Morgan James published authors with live and online events and audiences whom will benefit from their expertise.

Printed in the USA
CPSIA information can be obtained
at www.ICGtesting.com
JSHW022210140824
68134JS00018B/964

9 781683 501435